THE ARTIST'S MODEL

Its Role in British Art from Lely to Etty

THE ARTIST'S MODEL
Its Role in British Art from Lely to Etty

ILARIA BIGNAMINI & MARTIN POSTLE

University Art Gallery, Nottingham
30 April – 31 May 1991

The Iveagh Bequest, Kenwood
19 June – 31 August 1991

1006255389 X

ISBN 0 9516215 1 3
Edited by Martin Postle and Joanne Wright
Catalogue designed and printed in Great Britain in 1991
by Chas. Goater and Son Ltd., Nottingham; reprinted in 1999 by Goaters Limited, Nottingham
© 1991 Nottingham University Art Gallery and 1999 Djanogly Art Gallery,
University of Nottingham

Cover
JOHAN ZOFFANY
The Academicians of the Royal Academy, 1771-2
Reproduced on the cover and elsewhere in the catalogue
by Gracious Permission of Her Majesty the Queen

Sponsored by

with an additional grant from
The Paul Mellon Centre for Studies in British Art

Catalogue reprinted 1999 with further support from
The Paul Mellon Centre for Studies in British Art

in association with

Contents

Acknowledgements

Many people have contributed towards making this exhibition possible. Among those to whom we owe a particular debt of gratitude are Joanne Wright, Director of the University Art Gallery, Nottingham, and Sebastian Edwards, Assistant Curator at the Iveagh Bequest, Kenwood, who were responsible for the supervision of much of the day-to-day organisation of the project. Without their hard work and dedication this exhibition certainly would not have been possible. Our warm thanks also go to Julius Bryant who not only oversaw the administrative side of things at Kenwood, but also contributed some fascinating material to the catalogue (see cat.91). Many institutions and museums have assisted our work. Our thanks go particularly to Ann Chumbley of the Turner Collection at the Tate Gallery, Christopher Lloyd, Surveyor of the Queen's Pictures, Evelyn Newby of the Paul Mellon Centre, Sheila O'Connell of the Department of Prints and Drawings, British Museum, William Schupbach of the Wellcome Library, and Jehannine Mauduesch, Mary Anne Stevens and Helen Valentine of the Royal Academy of Arts. Among those who gave particular help along the way we would like to thank Louise Berg, Penny Buki, Richard Charleton-Jones, Juliette Foy, Anne French, John Jacob, Stephen Lloyd, Kim Sloan, Alastair Smart, John Sunderland, Catherine Whistler, and Basil Yamey. To Douglas Smith, who took many of the photographs reproduced in the catalogue, we owe a special thanks. We would like to express our special gratitude to a number of individuals who took an active part in preparing the catalogue, Monique Kornell, in addition to writing her own entry (cat.90), generously shared her own specialised knowledge with us and contributed greatly to the section on anatomy. Nicholas Alfrey, Brian Allen and Robin Simon also gave any amount of useful advice, as well as practical assistance in the preparation of the catalogue entries. We would like to thank Tracey Isgar, the assistant secretary at the University Art Gallery, Nottingham, who carried out a whole range of administrative tasks with a cheerful diligence which went far beyond the call of duty. Finally, we would like to thank Jacqui Jay Grafton and Albert Haynes for their expertise and patience in the production of this catalogue.

Ilaria Bignamini and Martin Postle

Foreword

The Artist's Model is an exploration of the way in which British artists employed the Life Model from the early-eighteenth to the mid-nineteenth centuries. It traces the origins of life drawing in the workshop of Sir Peter Lely in the 1670s, through the gradual acceptance of the practice as part of student training at the Royal Academy, to the less formal use of the artist's model in the studios of artists such as William Etty and David Wilkie. Among the questions the exhibition addresses are the changing roles of the male and female model, the role of the Life Model compared to classical statuary and the relationship between artistic study and scientific analysis of the human figure. It considers the fundamental artistic process of observation and interpretation, and provides a rare opportunity to compare artists of widely differing interests working on a common theme.

Over 90 paintings and drawings have been brought together for the exhibition and this has only been possible because of the generosity of our leaders whose support for the project we gratefully acknowledge here. We particuarly wish to express our thanks to Her Majesty the Queen for graciously agreeing to lend Zoffany's *Academicians*. A related work by Elias Martin has been lent from the National Academy in Stockholm and our Swedish colleagues must be thanked for the co-operation which has made this loan possible. Many of the works come from reserve collections and from private lenders and have never been shown in public before. We are especially grateful to David Alexander, Katrin Bellinger, Richard Constable, Ralph Holland, the Hon. Christopher Lennox-Boyd, John North, Mrs. A. Alfred Taubman, the Earl of Wemyss and March and other collectors who wish to remain anonymous, and are most appreciative of their willingness to live without their precious works for the duration of the show.

The energy and scholarship of Martin Postle who conceived the exhibition lies behind every aspect of its realisation. He, with Ilaria Bignamini, selected the loans and wrote the substantial catalogue. The publication has been generously sponsored by *Apollo Magazine* and by Christie's with financial assistance from the Paul Mellon Centre for Studies in British Art.

The Artist's Model continues a tradition of presenting scholarly studies of eighteenth- and nineteenth-century British art both at Kenwood and at the Nottingham University Art Gallery. It is, however, the first occasion on which these two institutions have collaborated and as such represents the starting point for a relationship which we look forward to developing when English Heritage relocates from London to Nottingham in Spring, 1994.

Joanne Wright
Director
Nottingham University Art Gallery

Julius Bryant
Head of Museums Division
English Heritage

THE ARTIST'S MODEL
from Lely to Hogarth

ILARIA BIGNAMINI

FROM the Renaissance onwards, the standard curriculum of the artist's training in Western countries revolved around three principle subjects: the Antique, the living model and the study of anatomy. Subjects such as technique, ornament, perspective, history and theory also played a crucial role in particular periods and contexts, but the Antique, the living model and anatomy always held a special position. They were taught by masters in their workshops and studios, and, from the sixteenth century, at academies of art (Pevsner, 1940; Boschloo et al., 1986-87). They played a central role in drawing books from the early seventeenth century (Bolton, 1985), and the core of visual culture provided from the Renaissance to the late nineteenth century. This essay will focus on specific aspects of the artist's approach to the model between 1673 and 1768 – from the creation of the first English academy for which documentation has survived, to the establishment of the Royal Academy of Arts.

The study of the Antique, the living model and anatomy is documented in the Dulwich College Album (ills. 1-2), which probably includes studies executed at the first English academy. The Academy of c.1673 (Talley, 1981, pp.308-309; Bignamini, 1988B, 3) originated in Lely's studio, and was probably attended by William Gandy (cat.no.76), his friend, William Fever, the Irish Catholic portrait-painter Garret Morphey and John Greenhill, whose name is associated with the Album (Stainton, 1987). George Freeman, a history and scene painter who practised as a drawing-master from about 1663, possibly was in charge of teaching, though it was Sir Peter Lely, then the foremost artist active in England, who supervised drawings executed by students there. It is probable that a number of these drawings are among the group of late seventeenth century drawings in the Album. These include studies after the Antique (ill.1) studies of the nude male and female models (ill.2), and a study of anatomy. Ill.1 shows a copy-drawing after an engraving made before the hands of the *Apollo Belvedere* were restored in 1532-33 (Haskell and Penny, 1981, p.148; Bober and Rubenstein, 1986, pp.71-2).

Until 1768, when the Royal Academy was established, the English academy was primarily a Life Class (cats. 2 and 4). This was true of the academies of c.1673 and 1692, the Academy in Great Queen Street (1711-20), the first St. Martin's Lane Academy (1720-24), Sir James Thornhill's Free Academy (1724-c.1731) and the second St. Martin's Lane Academy (1735-68) (Bignamini, 1988B, 3, 4 and 5). Outside London, early academies such as those of 1729 and 1760 in Edinburgh, 1742 in Dublin and 1754 in Glasgow and Birmingham were basically schools of design (Bignamini 1988A, pp.286-90, 360 ff. idem, 1989). At these academies students mainly

ill.1   Anon. *Apollo Belvedere, c.*1673
Red chalk on buff paper, 276 x 180 mm
Dulwich College Album, f. 3v. Dulwich College, London

executed copy-drawings after paintings, engravings and illustrations in drawing manuals, although the Life Class was important in Dublin (Denvir, 1983, pp.199-201).

The creation in London of the Academy attached to the Duke of Richmond's Gallery of Casts (1758-62) was an attempt to compensate for the lack of formal education in drawing from the Antique. Thus students who attended the Drawing School established by William Shipley in 1753 (Allan, 1968, pp.76-88; Bignamini, 1988A, pp.425-29) were taught the rudiments of drawing at Shipley's School, while they drew from the Antique at the Duke of Richmond's Academy and from the living model at the second St. Martin's Lane Academy. Yet some artists, Thomas Jones, for instance were dissatisfied with this 'tripartite' system, the precursor of the more comprehensive art school which came into being with the Royal Academy.

Another possibility for British artists to compensate for the deficiencies of art education in their country was to leave on the Grand Tour and visit Italy. Initially, however, it was mainly non-English artists who visited Italy. Some of them, including the German, Godfrey Kneller (cat.no.9) and the Frenchman Louis Chéron (cats.43 and 55), eventually settled in England and became involved with early academies of art. They imported teaching methods used in the studios of Dutch and Flemish masters and at continental academies, especially the *Accademia di San Luca* and the French Academy in Rome. However, an analysis of the drawings shows that those teaching methods failed to meet the needs of artists active in England. Immigrant artists had to adapt their draughtsmanship to the new context. Nevertheless, foreign and native artists together succeeded in laying the foundations of a common grammar for the visual arts. To understand the importance and implications of this transformation, we must return to Lely and the Academy of *c*.1673.

In general, academies of art can be divided into two principal categories: those created by the Prince or State as part of a system of cultural institutions designed to serve the policy of the central power, and those created by artists themselves in response to a growing market demand for art objects (Bignamini, 1986, 1986-87 and 1990). While the *Accademia del Disegno* (Florence, 1563), the *Accademia di San Luca* (Rome, 1593), and the *Académie Royale de Peinture et de Sculpture* (Paris, 1648) clearly fall within the first category, Dutch academies of the seventeenth century and early English academies fall within the second. It is a telling fact that the first English academy created in *c*.1673 seems to have been a response to the growing number of requests for apprenticeship addressed to Lely who was forced to develop an academy next to his studio. In the 1670s, as the London art market began to expand, the number of professional artists increased, and the studios of gifted and famous masters could not meet the demand. Academies (those of *c*.1673 and 1692), art clubs (the Virtuosi of St. Luke began to meet at London taverns in 1689), auction houses (the Vendu of 1692), drawing classes (at Christ's Hospital from 1692) and drawing schools (Bernard Lens II and John Sturt opened one in 1697) entered the scene in rapid succession. Although the picture is fragmentary, it nonetheless reveals the extent to which the arts were contributing to a more general transformation of English society. The dates of these various events correspond with the turning-points disclosed in recent studies of the growth of modern professions (Holmes, 1982) and the expansion of consumption in London (Earle, 1989).

Traditional forms of education (apprenticeship and studio

ill.2 Anon. *Female nude standing seen from behind, c.1673*
Black chalk, heightened with white on buff paper,
303 x 157 mm. Dulwich College Album, f. 21r.
Dulwich College, London

ill.3 GODFREY KNELLER (attrib.)
A slave seated in profile to left, after Annibale Carracci, c.1711
Black chalk on brown paper, 315 x 190 mm
BM 1897–8–13–9 (86v)
The Trustees of the British Museum

training) were not replaced by academies of art, but academies created the conditions for the elaboration of a common artistic vocabulary – a prerequisite for the birth of a national pictorial school. Workshops and studios separated artists from one another, and the results achieved were closely dependent on the ability of individual masters. At academies artists gathered together, working side by side from the same models under the guidance of the same instructor. Academies offered equal educational opportunities to a wide community of artists. This was especially valuable for artists living and working in a decentralised cultural context.

Academies are ideal centres from which to observe attitudes to the study of models and the gradual elaboration of a graphic vocabulary of drawing. For this reason, Academy studies rather than studio drawings have been singled out for special attention here. A comprehensive coverage of the period from Lely to Hogarth has not been attempted, because present knowledge of English academy drawing is still too fragmentary.

The two drawings selected to illustrate the activity of the Academy of c.1673 (ills.1 and 2) are not masterpieces, but they do convey an idea of the first moves towards the re-organisation of art teaching in this country. The most notable feature of seventeenth-century drawings in the Dulwich College Album is the emphasis on studies of the nude female model, demonstrated by black and red chalk drawings by various hands (see in particular folios 4r, 9v, 18v and 21r in the Album; photographs of the whole Album are preserved at The Paul Mellon Centre in London). The study of the female body, either in static and sensual poses (ill.2) or in action, was a principal pre-occupation. These studies were made in preparation for the depiction of female nudes in historical compositions (cat.12), for which there was almost no market in England.

From 1711 most artists of the developing English School had to adapt to the changing market demand, which was more sensitive to fashion than to style, and to public opinion and the press rather than to traditional art theory. Thus it was unlikely that teaching methods used in Europe, especially in Italian and French academies, could take root in this country, unless they were so modified as to be virtually new. For similar reasons, the emphasis on studies of the sensuality of the female body (ill.2 and cat.12) declined when their context (one of powerful courtiers and beautiful mistresses) ceased to exist.

When revived in 1711, the English academy was an unregulated educational institution, highly sensitive to market demand. Purchasers of paintings were interested, above all, in portraits of male and female sitters which did not require detailed studies of anatomy. Some knowledge of the Antique, of Old Master paintings, and of traditional poses was sufficient to meet the needs of many artists. This was certainly true of Sir Godfrey Kneller, the first Governor of the Academy in Great Queen Street. Three drawings (ills. 3-5) illustrate Kneller's attitude towards the model particularly well.

Kneller's *Slave seated* (fig.3; Stewart, 1983, p.174 no.76) is a sketchy copy of one of the captives beneath the *Perseus and Andromeda* fresco painted by Annibale Carracci on the ceiling of the gallery of Palazzo Farnese in Rome. Kneller's drawing reverses the original, which indicates that an engraving was the artist's model (for engravings after Annibale, see De Grazia, 1984, and Rome, 1986). The same applies to the study on the recto of the same sheet (Stewart, 1983, p.174, no.76, ill.114c), which is a finished drawing in reverse of another captive by Annibale (the same copied in Rome

ill.4   GODFREY KNELLER *Male nude seated to left, c.*1711
Black chalk on blue-grey paper 287 x 281 mm
BM 1888-7-19-71. The Trustees of the British Museum

ill.5   GODFREY KNELLER (attrib.)
Male nude seated, with drapery about his loins and forearm,
*c.*1711. Black chalk heightened with white, on blue-grey paper, 420 x 280 mm, BM 1897-8-13-9 (70).
The Trustees of the British Museum

ill.6   JOHN SMITH after GODFREY KNELLER
*Frances (Bennett), Countess of Salisbury, c.*1699
Mezzotint. The Trustees of the British Museum

from the original by Chéron, fig.7). Kneller's slaves, recto and verso, are reputed to have been made around 1665-75, before his visit to Rome. However, the two drawings are different in technique and purpose. The one on the recto is a finished red chalk drawing in which the student has attempted to be as faithful as possible to his model. That on the verso (ill.3) is a sketchy study in black chalk showing a mature artist freely adapting a pose derived from Annibale for some purpose other than mere reproduction. Moreover, the use of black chalk is common among artists who attended the Academy in Great Queen Street and the first St. Martin's Lane Academy, while red chalk was more widely used on the continent, both in studios and at academies of art. For these reasons, it seems likely that Kneller's *Slave* (ill.3) may have been made around 1711 to demonstrate to students how the Old Master tradition could assist the artist when working from the living model. Kneller's *Male nude seated* (ill.4; Stewart, 1983, p.170, no.57) gives substance to this hypothesis. The two drawings are similar in terms of the pose, the sketchy handling and the rendering of anatomy. Moreover, they suggest a similar attitude to the study of models. Kneller was satisfied with a study of the Antique and Old Masters and had a limited interest in anatomy. His purpose in drawing from the model was aimed principally at the study of poses.

It is hardly surprising, therefore, to find among Kneller's drawings an extraordinary example of the use of a male model (ill.5) in a pose typical of portraits of mourning female sitters (ill.6). The use of the male model as a substitute for the female was probably more widespread in studios and academies throughout Europe from the Renaissance to the late eighteenth century than is generally acknowledged. George Vertue's notebooks include a revealing description of model substitution as practised in Rome by the Flemish painter, Peter Angellis, in the late 1720s. Angellis, who was active in London from 1716 to 1728 and attended meetings of the Rose and Crown Club (Bignamini, 1988B, 2), went to Rome with the sculptors Laurent Delvaux and Peter Scheemakers in 1728, and studied there for three years. In Rome, Angellis had a 'young man that he made use of for his model to draw after – dressing him in several habits – or cloaths suteable to his purpose for his paintings at some times it causd much sport and laughter to his companions Artists when Angellis usd to dress up this young man (who was not very handsom nor likely) into womens dresses or habitts, he made such aukard – queere figures – that provok'd them to laugh at rather than admire, especially being a rustick ill shapd mortale and the cloath quite as ridiculous' (Vertue, III, p.105).

Painters like Kneller expected the academy to serve the interests of portraitists in the traditional vein. Drawings by other artist-members of the Academy in Great Queen Street suggest that Kneller's views were not shared by everyone. Jonathan Richardson's portrait of *Figg the Gladiator* (cat.69), for example, suggests that drawing from the living model ought to be directed towards the study of the individual model, rather than merely the rendering of poses such as those favoured by Kneller. A similar view was endorsed by Thornhill in 1729-31 when, objecting to standardized models available in copy-books, he undertook the project of publishing 162 studies of details from Raphael's *Cartoons* for the use of art students (Lambert, 1981, p.27, no.60). Hogarth, too, gave the female model a distinctly individual character (cat.56 and ill.17). Before such developments took place, however, a more rigorous approach to the model, and to the human figure in general, emerged in English academies.

ill.7 LOUIS CHÉRON
A slave crouching to left, his hands clasped behind his head, after Annibale Carracci, c.1676-77
Red chalk, touched with white, on buff paper
562 x 430 mm, BM 1953–10–21–11 (122)
The Trustees of the British Museum

ill.8 LOUIS CHÉRON
Male nude seated on a rock, turned to right, c.1676-77
Red chalk, heightened with white on buff paper
565 x 429 mm, BM 1953–10–21–11 (96)
The Trustees of the British Museum

Louis Chéron more than any other artist of the period was responsible for insisting on rigorous academy studies. He was a history painter and designer who was trained at the *Académie Royale de Peinture et de Sculpture* in Paris and at the French Academy in Rome before settling in England in 1695. Vertue (III, p.22) wrote that Chéron 'was much immitated by the Young people' who attended the Academy in Great Queen Street. Moreover, his academy nudes were engraved until 1735 (cat.42). Chéron was also responsible, with John Vanderbank, for establishing the first St. Martin's Lane Academy.

Two large albums of drawings executed by Chéron in Rome and in London are preserved in the British Museum (Croft-Murray and Hulton, 1960, pp.272-820). They form a unique collection of academy drawings covering a period of almost half a century, c.1676-1724, and document the artist's activities at three academies: the French Academy in Rome, the Academy in Great Queen Street and the first St. Martin's Lane Academy. They provide an excellent opportunity to examine Chéron's attitude to the model. Such a study is uniquely valuable, because the work of other artists active in the period is so widely dispersed. Consequently, Chéron's academy nudes provide the focus of attention here.

Copies of the *Captives* by Annibale Carracci which had caught Kneller's attention are among the drawings executed by Chéron in Rome. But whereas Kneller had used engravings as his models, Chéron made copies from the originals in the course of his training at the French Academy (Croft-Murray and Hulton, 1960, p.282, nos.122-24). Like Kneller (ills. 3 and 4), Chéron adapted his copy-drawings to studies of the living model, but with very different results. A comparison between Chéron's *Slave crouching to the left* (ill.7) and his *Male nude seated on a rock* (ill.8) shows the extent to which the artist had been taught to look at the living model through the eyes of the Old Masters. Anatomical features of the male body were closely derived from Annibale's *Captives*. Similarly, the features of the female body were derived from Raphael (ill.9), as the detail shown here, from Raphael's *Wedding Feast of Cupid and Psyche* on the vault of the loggia of the Farnesina in Rome, demonstrates.

Naked female models were forbidden at the *Académie Royale de Peinture et de Sculpture* throughout the seventeenth and eighteenth centuries, and to employ them in studios was extremely expensive (Rubin, 1977, p.22). Chéron therefore based his ideas of female anatomy on the Antique and on Old Master paintings, especially those of Raphael. The extent to which Chéron's treatment of the female body was influenced by the ideas he formed in Rome, is shown by drawings such as his *Nude female standing to right* (ill.10), a life study executed at the first St. Martin's Lane Academy in 1720-24. Even when working from the living model, Chéron could not distance himself from Raphael in the rendering of the body and the face. That particular face, which is repeated with only a few variations, in all his female studies was a 'mask' ultimately derived from Raphael, which is also to be found in a number of drawing books of the seventeenth and eighteenth centuries (Bolten, 1985).

Chéron imported into England teaching methods in use at academies in both Paris and Rome, but not all of these were accepted, or even approved, by the community of artists meeting in Great Queen Street and St. Martin's Lane. Vertue tells us that his copy-drawings and academy studies were much admired. Yet, his drawing style was criticised by Vertue as being 'generally heavy' (Vertue III, p.22). Nevertheless, his expressive rendering of anatomical features appealed to those artists who, like Chéron

ill.9 LOUIS CHÉRON
Pan and other deities at the marriage feast of Cupid and Psyche, after Raphael, c.1676-77
Red chalk on buff paper 562 x 430 mm
BM 1953–10–21–11 (109)
The Trustees of the British Museum

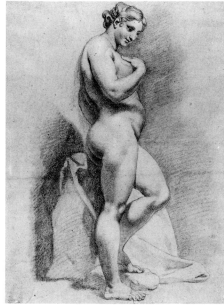

ill.10 LOUIS CHÉRON
Female nude standing to right, c.1720-24
Black and red chalk, heightened with white, on grey paper
590 x 413 mm, BM 1953–10–21–11
The Trustees of the British Museum

himself, found employment as book illustrators: according to Vertue, these included artist-members of the Academy of 1711 like Bernard Baron, Joseph Sympson (later a print-seller), John Vanderbank and Gerard Vandergucht, all of whom 'benefitted much of his drawing' (Vertue III, p.22).

Chéron's treatment of anatomy was more problematical, for it led to a degree of standardization which was at odds with the preference of artists like Richardson, who insisted on studies of individual character. Standardization was justified in the context of Court or State patronage which offered employment to many history painters and decorators. It also met the requirements of a number of designers active in England. It did not, however, suit many portraitists and illustrators of modern histories and novels. The depiction of individual character was more appropriate to their needs, and was regarded as more suitable in a society increasingly influenced by middle-class ideals. Moreover, Chéron's standardized anatomical features were too overtly shaped on 'foreign' models – Annibale Carracci for the male, and Raphael for the female body, a preference dictated from the seventeenth century onwards by trends in the collecting of Old Master drawings in France, which contributed to the creation of the aesthetic and educational strategy of the *Académie* at the time when Chéron was a student in Paris and Rome.

Chéron modified his approach to depicting male anatomy after he settled in England. This change was assisted, if not actually caused, by contact with William Cheselden who attended the first St. Martin's Lane Academy between 1720 and 1724 (cat.74). A leading surgeon and lecturer in anatomy, Cheselden was the author of two books illustrated with anatomical plates: *The Anatomy of the Humane Body* of 1713, and *Osteographia, or The Anatomy of the Bones* of 1733 (Bignamini, 1988B, 4; Kemp, forthcoming). His *Anatomy*, although very successful, was not a beautifully illustrated book. Indeed, he was so keenly aware of this deficiency that he commissioned new plates from Gerard Vandergucht (an artist-member of the Academy of 1711), some of which he included in the 1722 edition. Thus, during the very period of his attendance at the Academy, new anatomical illustrations to his book were being produced under his supervision. Cheselden was the first anatomist to instruct artists and art students in England. A comparison between two of Chéron's life-drawings of 1720-24 (ills.11 and 13) and two plates eventually published in Cheselden's *Osteographia* of 1733 (ills.12 and 14) demonstrates how much the anatomist contributed to the change in the artist's approach to depictions of the male nude.

The skeleton, virtually absent from drawings of Chéron's Roman period (ill.8), now became the visible structure supporting the whole body and its individual parts. The muscles, unrelated to the skeleton in drawings of the Roman period, and still over-emphasised in drawings of 1711-20, reveal the artist's knowledge of the most up-to-date anatomical research. The model's head, a mere 'mask' in drawings of the Roman period, but already a recognizable face in the later drawings, gained in characterisation and also expression. The outline of the body, especially the shoulders and torso, reflect the rendering of those same parts in contemporary anatomical illustrations. By the early 1720s, Chéron's rendering of the male nude was less concerned with art, with illusion and the past, and more with science, with reality and the present.

The situation was different with regard to the rendering of the female body. The nude female model clearly posed before the artist's meeting at the Academy of c.1673 (ill.2), but this was a studio-

ill.11   LOUIS CHÉRON
Male nude seated, leaning to right and looking up, his right arm raised, c.1720-24
Black chalk, heightened with white, on grey paper
650 x 556 mm, BM 1953–10–21–11 (84)
The Trustees of the British Museum

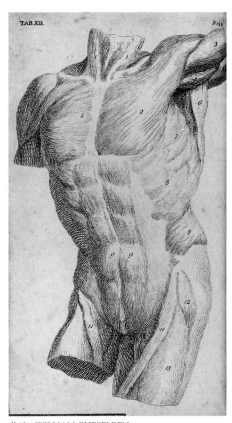

ill.12   WILLIAM CHESELDEN
Osteographia, 1733, pl.XII
By permission of the British Library

13

academy attended by only a few artists. In 1720, when drawing from the female model was introduced more regularly, artists were ill-equipped to handle the treatment of her form. Most English-born and immigrant artists who attended the Academy of 1720 had never before made studies of the nude female model.

Female models appear to have been employed occasionally in Italy and Germany at an early date. In general, however, the nude female model was introduced at academies on a regular basis only during the nineteenth century. England was an exception. The female model was regularly employed at the Academies of 1720-24 and 1735-68, and at the Royal Academy. It is possible that the decision to introduce the female model at the first St. Martin's Lane Academy was motivated by the same enthusiasm for anatomy and science which had encouraged the new approach to the rendering of the male nude in artists like Chéron. However, c.1761, William Hogarth expressed the alternative view that the female model was introduced in St. Martin's Lane 'to make it more inviting to subscribers' (Kitson, 1966-68, p.93).Whether or not this statement was made entirely seriously, some of his drawings certainly suggest that the study of the nude female model was a turning-point in his training as an artist. His female nudes were a new departure for the English School, and many of his ideas on beauty were derived from studies of the female form. A comparison between Chéron's and Hogarth's studies of female models is instructive.

At that time, illustrations of female anatomy did not exist, except for plates showing the reproductive organs. Female anatomy was usually derived from the Antique and from Old Master paintings (ills.9 and 10). But poses were also derived from drawing books. By the mid eighteenth century, these included summary plates showing a wide range of poses previously published individually, or in different combinations, in copy-books issued from the seventeenth century – one such example is Bernard Lens' drawing book of 1750. Some of the poses of the female model illustrated in this book are close to poses in academy studies by Chéron (ill.16) and Hogarth (cat.56), both of whom attended the first St. Martin's Lane Academy, Chéron as Director, and Hogarth as a student.

A comparison of Chéron's *Female nude seated to front* of c.1720-24 (ill.15) with Hogarth's *Female nude seated* (cat.56) also made in around 1720-24, clearly indicates two markedly different approaches to the same model. Chéron depicts a stereotyped face and statuesque figure in which the model's breast is unrelated to the twist of the body. Hogarth, on the other hand, depicts the features naturalistically, and the softer body surface is concerned with the expressive rendering of the individual model's abdomen, waist and breast. Hogarth's interest in a sensuous treatment of the female body in the mid-1730s can also be seen in the *Female nude* (ill.17), which he eventually used for the seated woman on the right in the *Pool of Bethesda* (1735-37), St. Bartholomew's Hospital, London. Here, the drawing reveals a body that is truly feminine. Moreover, Hogarth's model focuses attention on her breast, pressing the thumb of her right hand on to the nipple. This gesture seems like a polemical response to Chéron's 'sculptured' breasts, and to gestures associated with ideal female models of classical antiquity and the Italian Renaissance. *The Venus de Medici* points the middle finger of her right hand at the nipple, but she does not touch it, and thus, does not disturb the ideal shape of the female breast. Raphael's female models open their fingers on the nipple in a gesture associated with breast feeding, which is ultimately linked to the images of Sainted motherhood. With her thumb pressing on the nipple, Hogarth's model demonstrates that the greatest achievement for the artist is

ill.13   LOUIS CHÉRON
Male nude seen from behind, kneeling with arms raised,
c.1720-24. Black chalk, heightened with white,
on grey paper 654 x 565 mm, BM 1953–10–21–11 (83)
The Trustees of the British Museum

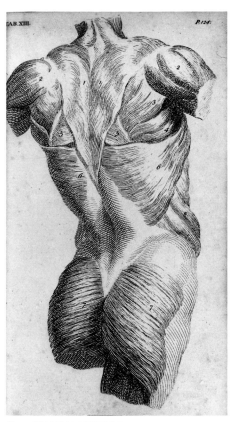

ill.14   WILLIAM CHESELDEN
Osteographia, 1733, pl.XIII
By permission of the British Library

the naturalistic rendering of a truly feminine body. 'The skin', Hogarth wrote in his *Analysis of Beauty* 'thus tenderly embracing, and gently conforming itself to the varied shapes of every one of the outward muscles of the body, soften'd underneath by the fat ... is evidently a shell-like surface ... form'd with the utmost delicacy in nature; and therefore the most proper subject of the study of every one, who desires to imitate the works of nature, *as a master should do*, or to judge of the performances of others *as a real connoisseur ought*' (Burke, 1955, p.75).

By the time Hogarth's *Analysis of Beauty* was published in 1753, the conventions for figure drawing in Britain were well-established. Many elements and many artists had contributed to their formulation. Private, unregulated, and artist-dominated academies active in London from 1673 to 1768 were centres where a cosmopolitan community of artists met to work from the same models. Old Master paintings, scientific anatomy, and a study of living models were the principal elements of their new graphic vocabulary. The result was a great fluency in drawing from the model, a remarkable naturalness in the rendering of the human figure, and a marked informality of the poses. These qualities were retained well after Hogarth's death. However, after the mid 1750s the Antique took the lead in greater measure. A new approach to the Antique changed the syntax of the body, and encouraged British artists to contribute to the formulation of a common European language for the arts.

ill.15   LOUIS CHÉRON
Female nude seated to front, c.1720-24
Black chalk, heightened with white, on grey paper
600 x 450 mm, BM 1953–10–21–11 (67)
The Trustees of the British Museum

ill.16   BERNARD LENS
A New and Compleat Drawing-Book, London 1751
Witt Library Collection

ill.17   WILLIAM HOGARTH *Female nude seated, c.1735*
Black and white chalk on brown paper, rubbed and slightly
stained with oil, 373 x 287 mm, RL 13482
Royal Library, Windsor Castle

THE ARTIST'S MODEL
from Reynolds to Etty

MARTIN POSTLE

British artists who studied at public academies in Rome and Paris in the mid-eighteenth century must have been continually aware of the advantages which these cities offered to students and practicing artists, as the following extract from a letter by a 'young artist' to the *Morning Chronicle* indicates: 'Last night I went for the first time, to the Academy of the Louvre, just to look on, where there were at least 200 students in a large hall ... all copying from a living man, who was placed naked in a reclining posture. The room is illuminated above the object by a very large lamp, with a dozen or twenty different flames. There are two rows of benches round the room; the highest for the statuaries, the other for the painters; every one has his own light placed at his right hand, with a screen between it and the object ... there are students here from all parts of the world ...' (*Morning Chronicle*, 1-3 May 1764). The unpretentious quarters of the St. Martin's Lane Academy must have seemed very homespun by comparison.

By the early 1750s, despite Hogarth's contempt for the highly regulated and hierarchical French Academy, many of his peers felt compelled to organise life drawing in England on continental principles. Their intention was partly to provide a more rigorous structure but also to establish a recognised theoretical basis on which to ground the teaching of students. Progress over the next few decades was swift. The first formal attempt to encourage a more uniformly academic style among students was made in 1759 by the Society of Arts which offered premiums 'for Drawings of Human figures from Living Models, at the Academy of Artists in St. Martin's Lane, in chalks, by young men under 24 years, to divide 30 Guineas'. John Hamilton Mortimer (1740-79) was among those young artists who featured consistently among the medal winners at the Society of Arts from 1769 to 1792 (see Allan, 1968, pp.215-17). An indication of Mortimer's skills, and the qualities sought by the Society can be seen in several life drawings, including the one shown here (ill.1), contained in an album at the Society of Arts. The same album also contains not only life drawings by other artists but competition drawings from the casts made at the Duke of Richmond's sculpture gallery (ill.2), which had opened in March 1758. As Benjamin Ralph noted in 1759, it was hoped that 'the study of these most exact copies from antiques may greatly contribute toward giving young beginners of genius an early taste and idea of beauty and proportion; which when thoroughly acquired will in time appear in their several performances' (Ralph, 1759, p.B).

Although the Duke of Richmond's Sculpture Gallery provided an increased opportunity to study antique statuary, it was with the foundation of the Royal Academy in 1768, and the integration of

ill.1   JOHN HAMILTON MORTIMER
Seated Male Nude Premium Drawing (2nd Prize), 1760
black chalk on paper, Royal Society of Arts

facilities for drawing from the life and the Antique, that the direct comparison of statuary with the living model became a vital issue. In 1767 the casts, benches, écorché figures and other paraphernalia of the St. Martin's Lane Academy were removed to new premises in Pall Mall. This building (previously an auction house) became, in 1769, the first headquarters of the Royal Academy. Life drawing was probably conducted on the top floor of the building, in a room lit by skylights, which also doubled as an exhibition space each Spring (Hutchison, 1956, pp.8-9). As early as 1771, however, more suitable quarters were found for the antique casts, the Life Class and the administrative headquarters of the Academy, in several disused royal apartments at Old Somerset House. In 1780 the Academy was moved to William Chambers's newly completed building on the same site (see cat.7).

The 'Rules and Orders' for the 'Academy of Living Models' and the 'Plaister Academy' were set out in January 1769. The organisation of the Antique Academy is outlined in cat.6. As far as the Life Class was concerned, it was decided that there should be two terms in the academic year. The 'Winter Academy of Living Models' was to run from Michaelmas (29 September) to April 9, and the 'Summer Academy' from 26 May to 31 August. The Winter Academy was to commence at 6pm, and the Summer Academy at 4pm. Originally it was specified that four male models were to be employed. In March 1769 it was also agreed that a female model should be employed 'three nights a week, every other week'. Male models sat for two hours, presumably maintaining a single pose during that time, aided by a staff or a rope suspended from the ceiling when necessary. This was the established practice in European academies. The porter, John Malin, who had previously worked at the Incorporated Society of Artists, also acted as a model receiving, in addition to his wage, two shillings and sixpence each time he sat (cat.70). The responsibility of acquiring models and supervising their use was settled on the Keeper of the Academy, George Moser (cat.46), who had previously performed this duty at the St. Martin's Lane Academy (Royal Academy, Council Minutes, 30 January 1769). Although it was Moser's job to supply models, any Academician was entitled to present models according to the Instrument of Foundation. Finally, it should be noted that female models were better paid than their male counterparts, for while male models received a wage of five shillings a week, with an additional shilling for each two-hour sitting, the female model received half a guinea per sitting.

In his first *Discourse* of January 1769 Reynolds had a good deal to say about the mistakes other Academies had made with regard to the use of the living model: 'The error I mean is, that the students never draw exactly from the living models which they have before them. It is not indeed their intention; nor are they directed to do it. Their drawings resemble the model only in the attitude. They change the form according to their vague and uncertain ideas of beauty, and make a drawing rather of what they think the figure ought to be, than of what it appears' (Reynolds, 1975, pp.20-21). Reynolds had himself drawn only infrequently from the model, although surviving drawings, such as the one illustrated here (ill.3), which relates to his painting *Garrick between Tragedy and Comedy* (Postle, November 1990, p.311) indicate that he was more proficient than some later commentators allowed (see for example Edwards, 1808, p.208). Reynolds encouraged students to observe the individual model closely and draw the figure with precision. 'The method I recommend', he added, 'can only be detrimental when there are but few living forms to copy ... but of this there is no

ill.2   RICHARD EARLOM
Paetus and Arria Premium Drawing (2nd Prize) 1760
black chalk on paper, Royal Society of Arts

danger: since the Council has determined to supply the Academy with a variety of subjects' (loc. cit.). Zoffany's *Academicians of the Royal Academy* (cat.5), painted shortly afterwards in 1771-2, included two of the Academy's models; a youth, who undresses in the foreground, and an older man, who is being positioned by the keeper, George Moser. The attitudes of both models are based on established types. The youth, although merely removing a stocking, takes up the attitude of the famous antique statue of the *Spinario* while the older man's pose is reminiscent of Renaissance paintings of *St. John the Baptist*, as that from the circle of Raphael which Zoffany subsequently included in *The Tribuna of the Uffizi* (Her Majesty the Queen).

Although he stressed the careful attention which students should pay to the model, Reynolds nevertheless believed that a drawing of the living figure ought not to be 'the representation of an individual, but of a class'. In this respect the model was to be treated no differently from the casts from which students drew in the Antique Academy. It was indeed a commonplace throughout the period to equate the study of the living model with statuary, as the following description by Reynold's pupil, James Northcote, indicates: 'The stillness, the artificial light, the attention to what they are about, the publicity even, draws off any idle thoughts and they [the students] regard the figure and point out its defects or beauties precisely as if it were clay or marble' (Northcote, 1830, p.102). In 1787 a man who had modelled at the Academy in Dublin was hanged for murder. The *Dublin Chronicle* (3rd November) recorded that the 'figure of this wretched culprit had been incomparable. It was between the Hercules and the Gladiator, and perhaps for size and symmetry in all its parts little inferior to the *Apollo Belvedere*', while in 1812 Benjamin Robert Haydon noted that his model had 'that extraordinary character perceived in the reclining figure (the Theseus) of the Elgin Marbles' (Elwin ed., 1950, p.168).

Although the rules which the Royal Academy established for the study of the model were generally accepted, not everyone appreciated the dogmatic nature of the teaching there. In 1773 an anonymous commentator (possibly the artist James Barry) wrote in a letter to the *Morning Post:* 'He [the student] learns to think, that a leg or arm cannot be graceful but in certain directions, that the head should have this inclination, and the body, that position, in order to present contrast. Cramped by such rule, without daring to express spontaneous feeling which may not be agreeable to it, he learns to produce actions as unnatural as if the figures were tied in the position. He looks no farther than his chalks, paper and model, and thinks the academy figure neatly finished and corrected according to the rule as the ultimatum he is to seek after'. (Barry, 1809, vol.1 p.228). The Academy's own Professor of Anatomy, William Hunter, had, in his lectures to the Royal Academy, also expressed reservations of a similar nature. 'In most pictures', he noted, 'there appears to me to be more composure, more inactivity, in the figures than we see in real life' (Kemp, 1975, p.43). The reason, he suggested, was that artists treated the living model like a cast: 'Most of the Ancient Statues which they copy and are taught to admire are figures in the quiet state of standing, sitting or lying down. And when they study life or Nature itself, they see it commonly in the same inactive state ... Is it unreasonable then to suppose that such easy and confined habits may introduce a quiet inactive manner in the figures and composition?' (op. cit., p.44). Although, it was not yet a major issue, the gap between those truths revealed by anatomy and those offered by the Antique was to widen considerably over

ill.3   Sir JOSHUA REYNOLDS
Seated female nude, c.1762, Private Collection on loan to the Royal Academy of Arts

succeeding years.

By the 1790s traits noted by Hunter and the anonymous correspondent in the *Morning Post* were evidently entrenched. John Williams who, under the pseudonym Anthony Pasquin, was a frequent critic of the Royal Academy, wrote in 1796 that it was 'the common lunacy of the day, among our junior artists, to claim the proud and high station of an Historical Painter, in the instant they can draw a figure in the Life Academy, with a decent analogy to truth ... '. (Pasquin, 1796, p.100). Pasquin's principal target was Benjamin West, by then President of the Royal Academy. 'The identity of Mr. West's figures' he noted, 'is so continually apparent, that I believe he has a few favourite domestics, who are the saints and demons of his necessities'; they had, moreover, 'the appearance of being drawn from the marble originals, and not the delicate and nearly imperceptible beauties of the nudity' (op. cit. p.10). To West however, the adaptation of classical statuary to the living model was not merely a question of convenience or habit, but the only viable means by which the human figure could transcend its inherent imperfect state – a conviction well demonstrated in his study of *Eve* based on the *Venus de Medici* (cat.29).

The evident distaste for a naturalistic depiction of the figure was especially manifest by the second half of the eighteenth century, in attitudes towards the female form. While West's *Eve* was promoted as an ideal, Rembrandt's prosaic treatment of the female nude was universally condemned in both France and England. In 1752 an English translation of Edmé-Francois Gersaint's catalogue of Rembrandt's etchings appeared in English. The introduction stated: 'whenever he introduces a naked figure in to his Compositions he becomes intolerable ... the ill Attitudes and Disproportion of his figures, especially of his women, render them extremely disgusting to a Person of True Taste' (quoted in White et al., 1988, p.6). And while Opie told students at the Royal Academy that were it not for the example of the Greeks 'we might have preferred ... the rank and vulgar redundance of a flemish or Dutch female' (Wornum ed., 1848, p.242), Haydon believed Rembrandt 'in the naked form, male or female was an Esquimeaux. His notions of the delicate form of women would have frightened an Arctic bear' (George, 1948, p.345).

The female model presented high-minded artists at the Royal Academy with several problems. First, as there was no established precedent for the use of the female model in European academies, there was no theoretical basis for instruction. Secondly, unlike male classical statuary which had been perennially classified and quantified, female physical perfection, as embodied in statues such as the *Venus de Medici* was far more subjectively considered. Finally, the low social status of female models was gravely at odds with the aura which surrounded their mythological counterparts. Male models, chosen principally for their musculature and physique, were often pugilists or soldiers (see cat.72). As such they were respected as individuals whose athletic appearance echoed the classical heroes with whom they were compared. Female models, by way of contrast, were regarded with curiosity and suspicion, especially as many were also prostitutes. J.T. Smith, for example, recalled how a woman named Mrs Lobb, who ran a brothel in Dyot Street, supplied Nollekens with models (Smith, 1878, vol.1, p. 356-7). James Northcote described the woman who sat to Reynolds for his painting *Cimon and Iphegenia* (Her Majesty the Queen) as 'a battered courtesan', noting how those female models who also worked as prostitutes 'looked upon it [modelling] as an additional disgrace to what their profession imposed upon them, and as something

ill.4 JOHN ROSSI after Joseph Nollekens
Seated Venus marble, National Trust, Petworth

19

unnatural, one even wearing a mask' (Northcote, 1830, p.103). It is not therefore surprising to discover that the female model who sat to James Barry in the late 1770s and early 1780s while he was working at the Society of Arts insisted that the artist paid her directly so that she could retain her anonymity (Pressly, 1981, p. 215, and 17).

The issue of morality in relation to the study of the naked figure became increasingly important during the later part of the eighteenth century. As early as 1775 Barry noticed 'the prejudices that many people have to naked figures, as indecent and tending to lewdness'. He expressed the belief that women were even more hypocritical in their attitudes towards nudity than men 'and discover what they would wish to conceal by their affected squeamishness and over delicacy in this respect' (Barry, 1775, p.155). The Royal Academy which, unlike the St. Martin's Lane Academy, acted as a regulating body, was increasingly made aware of its responsibility to the public as well as to artists. In 1780, for example, when the first Academy exhibition was held in William Chamber's New Somerset House, it bowed to public pressure exerted through the pages of the popular press and agreed to attach fig leaves to the genitalia of the male statuary, which was then available for inspection by visitors to the annual exhibition (Postle, June 1990, p.290). Several years later the *Morning Herald* (9th May 1785), in a scathing attack on Reynolds' *Venus and Cupid* (unlocated) made it clear that studying the living model was *per se* a moral as well as an aesthetic issue. 'Sir Joshua Reynolds', it observed, 'will not suffer in his moral character by any charge of having painted his Bacchante, called by error a Venus, from life, as there is traced in every figure shop in London the plaster cast of a model of a French artist, from which Sir Joshua painted his wanton'.

Despite an unremitting attachment to the Ideal at the Royal Academy and public disquiet at naturalistic representation of the nude, there was, by the 1790s, evidence of an increased interest in the less doctrinaire attitudes to the study of the model. James Barry, a Visitor in the Academy Schools during the 1790s, produced a number of drawings of the reclining female model, which reveal a strong interest in relaying the characteristics of the unidealised female form (cat.58). Similarly, Joseph Nollekens in 1800 made a clay *modello of Venus* (Lord Egremont) which he based on his studio model as she sat to put on her stockings after an 'official' sitting. According to J.T. Smith, the figure was greeted with guarded scepticism: 'It was the opinion of most artists, that many parts of this figure could have been much improved: they thought the ankles unquestionably too thick; and that to have given it an air of the antique, the right thigh wanted flesh to fill up the ill formed nature which Nollekens had strictly copied. The abdomen was far from good; and the face was too old, and of a common character, but the back was considered extremely beautiful' (Smith, 1828, vol.2, p.64). Neveretheless, Nollekens himself, when a Visitor at the Royal Academy Schools, posed the female model in this same attitude (op. cit., p.65). His *modello* of Venus was originally bought by the Earl of Carlisle who intended to have a marble statue made from it to show at Castle Howard. However, his family objected and it was eventually bought, after Nollekens' death, by Lord Egremont. The very fact that Egremont commissioned an exact replica in marble from John Rossi (ill.4) and instructed the sculptor to retain all the idiosyncracies of the clay figure, surely indicates that the appeal of the statue lay precisely in its naturalism rather than any adherence to the received classical canon of female beauty.

Nollekens was only one of a number of Visitors, at the turn of the century, who attempted to engender a more innovative approach

ill.5 Sir DAVID WILKIE
Seated Male Nude c.1807-8, Private Collection

ill.6 BENJAMIN ROBERT HAYDON
studies of feet inscribed: my own foot, Venus
Department of Prints and Drawings, British Museum

towards the model at the Academy. Henry Fuseli, for example, allowed students to adopt a much freer approach to drawing the model and himself produced a number of rapid pen and wash sketches of the model (cats. 60a and 60b). He also encouraged the young William Etty to paint directly from the figure in oils, a practice which Etty continued, both in the Schools and in his studio, for the remainder of his career (see cats.1, 14, and 15).It was partly as a result of the innovations of artists such as Fuseli and Nollekens at the turn of the nineteenth century, that the generation of artists who came through the Academy Schools including Benjamin Robert Haydon and David Wilkie, adopted a far more empirical attitude towards the model. Wilkie, who arrived in London from Scotland in 1805 (see cats.19 and 63), was even in the habit of using himself as a model, as Haydon recalled: 'I went to his room rather earlier than the hour named, and to my utter astonishment found Wilkie sitting stark-naked on the side of his bed, drawing himself by the help of a looking glass! "My God Wilkie" said I, "where are we to breakfast?". Without any apology or attention to my important question, he replied: "It's jest copital practice [sic]"' (Elwin, 1950, p.36). The drawing by Wilkie shown here (ill.5), is the only putative example of Wilkie's use of himself as a naked model. Not only are the features of the model clearly those of Wilkie (which he often included in his own genre paintings), but the figure seems to be holding a piece of chalk in his left hand. Haydon too, although apparently taken aback at the extreme nature of Wilkie's practice, also made drawings from his own hands and feet (ill.6), as the many surviving drawings contained in albums in the British Museum indicate.

In the early years of the nineteenth century, Haydon constantly sought new ways to reconcile the study of the Antique with the living model although, before he had seen the Parthenon sculptures, he was continually perplexed by the differences between the two. He wrote in 1807, 'In my model I saw the back vary according to the action of the arms. In the antique these variations were not so apparent. Was nature or the antique wrong? Why did not the difference of shape from difference of action appear so palpably in the antique as in nature? This puzzled me to death' (Elwin, 1950, p.75). In 1810, by which time he had made a careful study of the Parthenon sculptures, Haydon made a cast from a young black model named Wilson (see cat.68), whom he drew frequently (ill.7), and described as 'a perfect antique figure alive' (op. cit., p.123). The intention was to demonstrate to himself the close similarity between the living form and the best classical statuary. Having built a wall around the model he was, 'put into a position, extremely happy at the promise of success as he was very proud of his figure. Seven bushels of plaster were mixed at once and poured in till it floated him up to the neck. The moment it set it pressed so equally upon him that his ribs had no room to expand for his lungs to play and he gasped out, "I - I - I die"'. The model survived and the cast was, according to Haydon, 'the most beautiful cast ever taken from nature' (ibid., p.124).

The antique was important to Haydon in so far as it reinforced what the artist has already learnt by the study of the living model and anatomy. Indeed when he formed his 'school' in 1815 (see cats. 79, 84 and 85) anatomy lay at the very root of his teaching and was not merely an adjunct to other activities. Although anatomy had been studied by British artists since the seventeenth century it underwent a significant revival during the late-eighteenth and early-nineteenth centuries – as the presence of the extraordinary écorché figure of James Legg in the present exhibition indicates

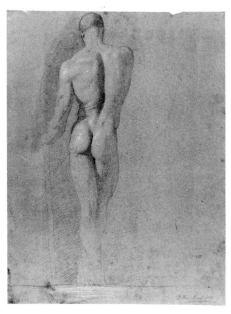

ill.7 BENJAMIN ROBERT HAYDON
Standing male nude, inscribed: *Wilson, 10 Decʳ 1810*
Department of Prints and Drawings, British Museum

(cat.91). By the second half of the eighteenth century, a number of British artists cultivated a serious interest in anatomy. Foremost among these was George Stubbs (1724-1806), whose expertise was such that by his mid-twenties he was already giving private instruction to medical students in York (although his activities attracted suspicion in some quarters). Around 1759 Stubbs began work on his greatest achievement, *The Anatomy of the Horse*, published in 1766, although it was not until after the mid-1790s that he produced a series of drawings based on dissection from the human body (ill.8). Although these drawings were never engraved (they are now in the possession of the Worcester Free Public Library, Massachusetts and the Yale Center for Studies in British Art) they were part of an intended work entitled *A Comparative Anatomical Exposition of the Human Body with that of a Tiger and a Common Fowl*.

Stubbs' interest in anatomy went far beyond that of any British or European artist of the period in its intensity, its reliance on empirical methods of research, and most of all, its appreciation of anatomy for its own sake. He was not alone, however, in believing that a true knowledge of anatomy could only be gained by first-hand experience. John Russell (cat.87) and John Flaxman (cats. 82 and 88), for example, both cultivated an interest in anatomy which went beyond the bounds of accepted convention. It was not however until the early-nineteenth century that artists began to conceive of anatomy, as an alternative, and not merely a supplement, to the study of the Antique. The growth of artistic interest in anatomy was paralleled, and indeed heavily influenced, by the interest of a number of anatomists in the visual arts, notably the Scots surgeons John and Charles Bell. The Bells were gifted draughtsmen as well as highly skilled surgeons, and included their own illustrations for their books on anatomy, such as the plate illustrated here (ill.9) from John Bell's *Engravings explaining the anatomy of the bones, muscles and joints* of 1794. Haydon bought a copy of this book in 1804 (see Munby, 1937, pp.345-7), which he admired for its 'admirable perspicuity', and more surprisingly, its 'beauty' (Elwin, 1950, p.21). The significance of the Bells' books, and of Charles Bell's lectures to art students in the early years of the nineteenth century, was that they showed artists that direct observation, dissection and drawings made from the human figure, were of greater use, if less tasteful, than the idealised, stylized, and rather sanitized depictions of human anatomy, which were slavishly copied from Albinus and Vesalius, such as the carefully delineated example shown here by John Singleton Copley (ill.10).

Among the first artists in the nineteenth century to elevate the status of anatomy in his own artistic education above that of the Antique was the Scots miniaturist Andrew Robertson (1777-1845), who left some very illuminating accounts of his time in the Royal Academy Schools in 1801-2 (see Robertson ed., 1895, p.46 ff). As there was evidently little anatomical instruction within the Academy (the incumbent Professor of Anatomy, John Sheldon having all but ceased to perform his duties), Robertson subscribed to a series of lectures held by Joshua Brookes in Blenheim Street, where he was able to observe and perform dissections, 'I have', he noted in a memo of January 1802, 'been dissecting some time - 3 of us at a subject - shall dry the bones and keep the skeleton' (op. cit., p.63). In March 1802, Robertson moved from the Antique Academy to the Life Schools of the Royal Academy, the first of his peers, he claimed, to make the transfer. He attributed his success not to his facility in drawing from the cast but from his extra-curricular anatomical research, which he stated was 'the most useful thing in

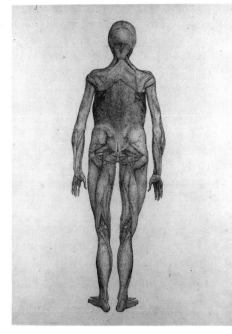

ill.8 GEORGE STUBBS
Drawing of a Human Body for the plate in
'A Comparative Anatomical Exposition of a Human Body
with that of a Tiger and a Common Fowl' 1804-06
British Art Center, Yale

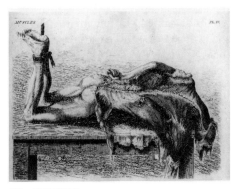

ill.9 JOHN BELL
Plate IV from 'Engravings explaining the anatomy of the bones,
muscles and joints', etching with engraving, Edinburgh 1794
Book 2, facing p.109

drawing from life, for action is so momentary' (ibid., p.63). Although there is not space here to explore all the ramifications of the growth in importance of anatomy in relation to the study of the living model in the early-nineteenth century, it is essential to stress that the role of anatomy in artistic education was a deeply divisive issue and one which polarised radical and conservative elements in British artistic circles.

This issue came to a head over the publication of an article in *The Artist* on 4 July 1807 by the surgeon Anthony Carlisle, who suggested that an understanding of anatomy was not essential to an artist's training (see also Farington, VIII, p.3789). In the same article he implied that 'certain anatomists' were seeking 'more influence in the fine arts than their studies can justly claim'. This was an indirect attack on Charles Bell who at the time was renowned for the lectures and demonstrations he gave at his home in Leicester Street to artists, including Haydon and Wilkie. The issue was all the more contentious as Carlisle and Bell were then rivals for the impending election of a new Professor of Anatomy at the Royal Academy. Although Bell was far better qualified by virtue of his skills as a lecturer, his superiority as an anatomist, and his written work (including *The Anatomy of Expression in Painting* of 1806) he was ultimately unsuccessful – despite the support of Fuseli and Flaxman. Carlisle, who was duly elected Professor of Anatomy in 1808, clearly seemed a safer bet to the conservative lobby within the Academy, as Bell's letters of the period indicate (Bell, ed., 1870, p.119 ff.).

Bell's rejection by the Royal Academy was just one aspect of a growing concern with the burgeoning interest in more empirical ways of approaching the living model, which the art establishment felt undermined the canon on the Antique. In 1804 West had admonished students at a presentation ceremony at the Academy that proficiency was 'not to be gained by rushing impatiently to the School of the living Model; correctness of form and taste was first to be sought by an attentive study of the Grecian figures' (Hoare, 1805, p.182). West was also of the opinion that although under Fuseli's Keepership the students were given proper attention, the Schools as a whole were 'all in disorder' (Farington, VIII, p.3087). Conservative artists like Martin Archer Shee also voiced concern over the increasing inattention to the paradigm offered by the Antique. In his *Elements of Art* of 1809 he noted for example the 'general (and it is to be feared) growing disregard of that purity of form and character, of which the Greeks have supplied us with the most impressive examples, is alarming to the interests of Taste' (Shee, 1809, p.53). An added complication to the 'interests of Taste' was the presence in London of the Elgin Marbles, in Park Lane (see cats. 25 and 41) which ironically vindicated those who upheld the primacy of the study of anatomy and the living model over the Antique in the education of the artist.

Inconsistencies which Haydon had previously found when comparing his model with antique statuary were resolved when he examined the reliefs and free-standing sculptures from the Parthenon in 1808. Indeed, his reaction (see cat.25) was very similar to that of Charles Bell, who had first seen the Elgin Marbles in November 1807: 'There is', he wrote of one of the figures from the pediment, 'a massiveness and breadth in the laying out of the muscles, in the flatness of the thighs; there is fleshiness in the form of the joints, great strength in the twisting of the trunk ...' (Bell, ed. 1870, p.115). The figures from the Parthenon were far closer to the living model than any antique statuary hitherto discovered. Moreover, they proved, despite the notorious objections of Richard Payne Knight, to be genuine Greek Sculptures, and not merely

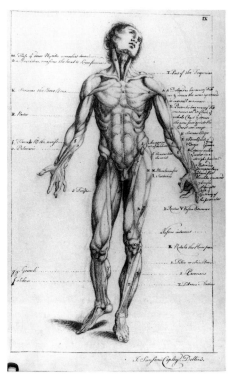

ill.10   JOHN SINGLETON COPLEY
Anatomical study, after Vesalius 1756, pen and ink on paper
Department of Prints and Drawings, British Museum

Roman copies of Greek originals like the *Venus de Medici* or the *Apollo Belvedere*. So impressed were artists and connoisseurs with the life-like aspect of the Parthenon sculptures that pugilists were employed to pose naked beside them, before selected audiences, in a variety of attitudes (see Farington, IX, p.3306).

The impact of the Elgin Marbles on the generally accepted relationship of the antique to the living model was profound, for they seemed to show that the greatest ancient sculptors had looked closely at the individual model, rather than seeking to establish a range of generalised archetypes. In 1814 Hazlitt, writing in *The Champion* stated, concerning Reynolds' 'inability to draw the naked figure', that 'drawing from the antique would not have enabled either him or anyone else to draw from the naked figure. The difficulty of copying from nature, or in other words of doing anything that has not been done before, or that is worth doing, is that of combining many ideas at once, or of reconciling things in motion: whereas in copying from the antique, you have only to copy still life, and in proportion as you get a knack at the one, you disqualify yourself for the other' (Hazlitt, 1933, vol.18, p.145). From the 1820s life drawings by British artists indicate (see cats. 62 and 63) that the model was viewed less as a poor relation to the Antique and more as an entity in its own right. The Antique was still attentively studied, although similarities between life drawings and those made from statuary decreased – as Wilkie's impromptu watercolour of his nude female model astride a ladder (ill.11), for example, illustrates. With this in mind, Turner's practice, when a Visitor in the Life School during the 1830s, of posing the female model with a cast of the *Venus de Medici* (cat.32) ought perhaps to be viewed less as a conscious attempt to introduce innovations to the Life Class but rather as a nostalgic attempt to recover past conventions.

ill.11   Sir DAVID WILKIE
Female nude ascending a ladder, pencil and ink on paper
Signed and dated July 18, 1840
Department of Prints and Drawings, British Museum

Colour Plate I   ? BRITISH SCHOOL, *A Life Class*, ? mid-19th century, Royal Academy of Arts, London (cat.3)

Colour Plate II – p.38

Colour Plate III ELIAS MARTIN, *The Cast Room at the Royal Academy*, exhibited 1770
Royal Academy of Fine Arts, Stockholm (cat.6)

Colour Plate IV   BRITISH SCHOOL, *The Antique School of the Royal Academy*, c.1780-83, Royal Academy of Arts, London (cat.7)

Colour Plate V   Sir GODFREY KNELLER, *Portrait of the Artist*, c.1670
Mrs A. Alfred Taubman (cat.9)

Colour Plate VI   Sir PETER LELY, *Sleeping Nymphs by a Fountain*, early 1650s
By permission of the Governors of Dulwich Picture Gallery (cat.12)

Colour Plate VII   WILLIAM ETTY, *Male nude, seated*, *c.*1815-18, Private Collection (cat.15)

Colour Plate VIII JOHN CONSTABLE, *Male nude, reclining, ? c.*1808-10, Private Collection (cat.17)

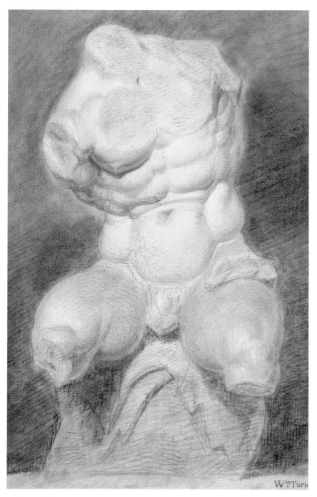

Colour Plate IX   J.M.W. TURNER, *Belvedere Torso*, c.1790-95
The Board of Trustees, Victoria and Albert Museum, London
(cat.18)

Colour Plate XI   JOHN CONSTABLE, *Male nude in the attitude
of Michelangelo's 'Jonah',* c.1800-01, The Board of Trustees
The Victoria and Albert Museum, London (cat.26)

Colour Plate X – p.50

31

Colour Plate XII   Attributed to FRANCIS WHEATLEY, *The Cast Room of the Royal Academy, c.1795-1800*
Trustees of the National Museums and Galleries on Merseyside, Lady Lever Art Gallery (cat.40)

Colour Plate XIII – p.66

Colour Plate XIV   Sir DAVID WILKIE, *Female nude, seated, c.*1833
The Visitors of the Ashmolean Museum, Oxford (cat.63)

Colour Plate XV   JOHN BOYNE, *A Meeting of Connoisseurs, c.*1807, The Board of Trustees,
Victoria and Albert Museum, London (cat.68)

Colour Plate XVI   J.M.W. TURNER, *Female nude, standing, c.1796-98*, The Turner Collection, Tate Gallery, London (cat.73a)

Colour Plate XVII   BRITISH SCHOOL, *William Cheselden giving an Anatomical Demonstration*, ? *c.*1733-35
Wellcome Institute Library, London (cat.74)

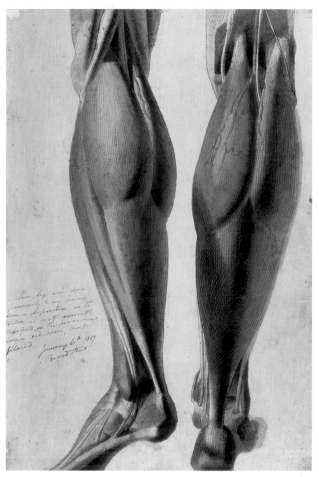

Colour Plate XIX   BENJAMIN ROBERT HAYDON,
Anatomical Drawing of Two Legs, 1805
Royal Academy of Arts, London (cat.84)

Colour Plate XVIII – p.85

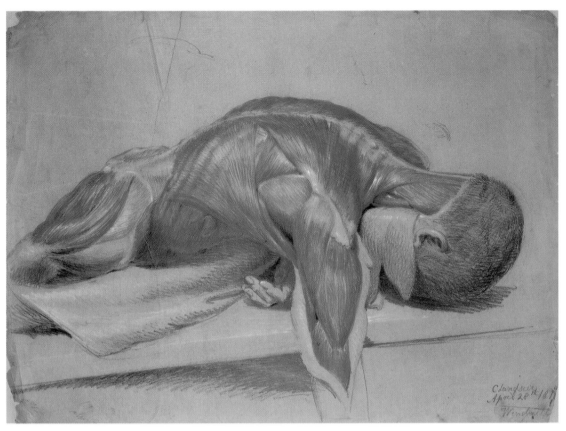

Colour Plate XX   CHARLES LANDSEER, *Cadaver, lying face down*, ? 1815, Wellcome Institute Library, London (cat.85)

Colour Plate XXI   After MICHAEL HENRY SPANG, *Écorché figure*
After 1761, The Board of Trustees, Victoria and Albert Museum, London
(cat.90)

I Artists and Models

The first section of the exhibition, which comprises 17 oil paintings, introduces the various ways in which artists approached the model in the 18th and early-19th centuries. One seminal aspect of this section is that for the first time all the major known paintings of British academies are shown together, from the earliest putative depiction of Sir Godfrey Kneller's Academy (cat.2), founded in 1711, to Zoffany's superb *Academicians of the Royal Academy* of 1771 (cat.5), and Elias Martin's *Cast Room at the Royal Academy* (cat.6), which has not been seen in England since it was first exhibited in 1770. This has, in itself, produced some surprises, including the identification of what may be the only known depiction of the St. Martin's Lane Academy (cat.4), as well as the discovery that a painting which was, until recently, thought to be an important record of an 18th-century academy, is in all probability a 19th-century fake (see cat.3). The role of allegory is illustrated by Medina's *Apelles and Campaspe* (cat.8), while the relevance of the nude model to history painting is brought out in Lely's *Sleeping Nymphs by a Fountain* (cat.12), the earliest work in the exhibition. The living model – both male and female – is also represented, notably in the oil studies of William Etty, the most prolific British painter of the nude, and in works by John Constable, whose abiding interest in the figure is often overlooked in the light of his reputation as a landscapist. Artists' portraits complete the section, including an early self-portrait of Sir Godfrey Kneller (cat.9), which serves to demonstrate the important role which antique statuary, prints, and anatomy, played in shaping attitudes towards the living model – themes which are taken up in subsequent sections of the exhibition.

Colour Plate II   JOHAN ZOFFANY *The Academicians of the Royal Academy*, exhibited 1772
Reproduced by gracious permission of Her Majesty the Queen (cat.5)

Female nude, standing   **1**

WILLIAM ETTY (York 1787-1849)

Oil on canvas; 208.3 x 118.7 cm
*c.*1825-30

PROVENANCE: J. McWhirter, London; presented to Bradford
City Art Gallery in 1921 by Mr & Mrs F. V. Gill in memory
of the late Alfred Gill

EXHIBITED: Burlington House, 1874; York Corporation Art
Gallery, 1911

LITERATURE: Farr, 1958, no.202, 'Standing Female Nude
(The Bather)'

Bradford Art Galleries and Museums

Although he was born and died in York, William Etty spent his
working life in London. At the age of nineteen he made a
series of drawings from the Antique at a plaster-cast shop in
Smithfield. He used these works as proof of his proficiency in
order to gain entry to the Royal Academy Schools, where he
was admitted on 15 January 1807 by the Keeper, Henry Fuseli.
In the same year he also began a twelve-month apprenticeship
with Thomas Lawrence. Etty's principal aspiration was to be a
history painter, and so, in accord with the accepted tenets of
High Art, he made the study of the living model the focus of
his activity – a concern which developed over the years into an
obsession. And it is as a painter of the nude that Etty is best
remembered today. Although the specified period of enrolment

at the Academy Schools at that time was ten years, Etty
returned to the life class regularly throughout his life, even
though his continual presence there attracted criticism from
some of his peers in later years (Farr, 1958, p.46). Etty painted
from the living model in private, as well as at the Academy (in
1830 he is recorded as renting a room in Soho Square expressly
for this purpose, op. cit., p.61). He also studied from the life in
academies in Europe, spending, for example, seven months at
the Venice Academy. There his fluent, assured, oil sketches
were so admired that he was made an honorary Academician a
full two years before he became an Associate Royal
Academician. It was also during his European sojourns (1816,
1822-3 and 1830) that Etty gained the opportunity to study at
first hand the Venetian old masters, Titian and Tintoretto,
whom he most admired, as well as the artist whose sensuous
handling of flesh tones his own work most resembles – Sir
Peter Paul Rubens.

By the mid-1820s Etty attracted criticism from certain
sections of the press because of the naturalism of his female
nudes. In January 1822, for example, *The Times* stated: 'Naked
figures, when painted with the purity of Raphael, may be
endured; but nakedness, without purity is offensive and
indecent, and in Mr. Etty's canvass (sic) is mere dirty flesh' (see
Farr, 1958, p.31). Etty was by nature quiet, undemonstrative,
and temperate (his favourite drink was tea). He remained a
bachelor throughout his life, and professed not to understand
the heated reactions elicited by his work. 'People may think
me lascivious,' he said, 'but I have never painted with a
lascivious motive. If I had, I might have made great wealth'
(Rose, 1942, p.28).

The attitude of the model in the present painting is loosely
related to the *Venus Pudica* (Haskell and Penny, 1981, cat.85),
a pose of classical pedigree which was often adapted to the
living model in the Royal Academy Schools. The work is
however highly unusual in that it is life size, unlike the
majority of Etty's academic studies. It is also on canvas rather
than millboard, the medium which Etty favoured in the Life
Class. This, and the fact that it is a 'companion' to a life-sized
male nude (Bolton Art Gallery, Farr, 1958, cat.204) suggests
that the picture was commissioned from Etty, and worked up
from a separate life-study.   M.P.

A Life Class (? Thornhill's Academy)   **2**

BRITISH SCHOOL

Oil on canvas, mounted on board, oval; 29.8 x 24.9 cm
*c.*1718-20

PROVENANCE: Unknown

EXHIBITED: Museum of London 1985 (277)

LITERATURE: Kitson, 1966-68, pl.43/2; Bignamini, 1988A,
pp.211-12, fig.52; idem 1988B, 3

Private Collection

The painting shows a large room with a dozen or so men seated
or standing round a table. Some of them are drawing from the
living model, who poses in an uncomfortable posture
reminiscent of the *Borghese Gladiator* – a classical statue well
known in England through copies and plaster casts since the
first half of the 17th century (Haskell and Penny, 1981, no.43
pp.221-24). Not all the artists in the room are portrayed in the
act of drawing. Some are painting, others are talking. Two casts
from the Antique stand on pedestals. The statue on the left is
reminiscent of the *Faun with Pipes* (Haskell and Penny, 1981,
no.38), while the female statue on the right is a *Venus*,
although it does not correspond directly to any particular
classical prototype.

This painting, for which no convincing attribution has so far been produced, shows an academy at work. Two London academies might be depicted in this picture: the Academy of 1711, which initially met in Great Queen Street and later, c.1718-20, at Sir James Thornhill's house in Covent Garden, or Thornhill's Free Academy established at the same address in 1724.   I.B.

A Life Class
? BRITISH SCHOOL

(COL PLATE I) **3**

Oil on canvas; 96.5 x 134.6 cm

PROVENANCE: Purchased by the Royal Academy in 1885

EXHIBITED: Royal Academy, 1908 (111); Guildhall, London, 1957 (28); Royal Academy, 1963 (2); Hampstead Arts Centre, 1966 (25); Royal Academy, 1968 (877); Museum of London, 1985 (281)

LITERATURE: Dobson, 1902, pp.55, 161, 183; id.,1907, p.61; Saxl and Wittkower, 1948, p.58; Phillips, 1964, pp.133 and 278, fig.135; Kitson, 1968, pp.65-66, and p.66, no.76, fig.1; Paulson, 1971, vol.1, p.370, fig.139; Murdoch, 1985, p.196, no.281; Bignamini, 1988A, pp.314-5, 349-54

Royal Academy of Arts, London

This painting was purchased by the Royal Academy of Arts in 1885, as a representation of the St. Martin's Lane Academy by William Hogarth. In 1963, when the picture was exhibited at the Royal Academy (no.2), it was suggested that it was not British but of French or Italian origin. However in 1964 it was still ascribed to Hogarth, when it was described as 'a valuable record of Hogarth's School in St. Martin's Lane' (Phillips, 1964, p.112). In 1966 Michael Kitson attributed the painting to the 'Circle of Hogarth,' and remarked that details in the painting matched Hogarth's own description of the Academy (Kitson, 1968, pp.65-66). Paulson, in 1971, confirmed that the painting was not by Hogarth but still stated that it portrayed the St. Martin's Lane Academy (Paulson, vol.1, p.370). In 1985, however, Tessa Murdoch once more raised the possibility that the Academy shown might not be British, but French or Italian (Murdoch, 1985, p.196). Throughout, a date of c.1740-50 was generally accepted.

In order to establish why the present painting was for so long accepted as the St. Martin's Lane Academy – or even as a contemporary representation of an 18th century Academy – one has to turn to Hogarth's own retrospective account of the founding of the St. Martin's Lane Academy. In his *Apology for Painters*, which he began to write around 1760, Hogarth left several clues as to the appearance of the Academy. He recalled that, on the death of his father-in-law, Sir James Thornhill, he had inherited the 'neglected apparatus' belonging to Thornhill's Academy, and had set up an Academy in St. Martin's Lane (Kitson, 1968, p.93). Referring to himself in the third person, Hogarth then stated that as 'a room big enough for a naked figure to be drawn after by thirty or forty people was necessary he proposed a subscription for hire of one in St. Martin's Lane and for the expenses attending in this was soon agreed to be sufficient number of artists he presented them with a proper table for the figure to stand on a large lamp iron stove and benches in a circular form ...' (op. cit., p.94). It was Hogarth's reference to the room which could seat thirty to forty people, together with the lamp, the 'proper table,' and the circular benches which prompted the supposition that this picture was indeed of the St. Martin's Lane Academy. The style of the painting was also, of course, curiously reminiscent of Hogarth.

The picture has been surface-cleaned for the present exhibition, and examined under ultra-violet light. It has revealed a paint surface which, although caked in a layer of thick brown varnish, is remarkably free from any traces of *pentimenti*. It has also highlighted a number of disturbing details. First, the lamp is slung from the ceiling by a slender rope. Oil lamps were not hung from the ceiling in this manner but fixed to the walls and ceiling by ties and metal brackets, as one can see in cats.4 and 6. Secondly, the lamp's extractor-pipe, which is supposed to expel smoke from the room, as in cat.4, is incorrectly drawn, and leads nowhere. (An extractor-pipe, if it is fed through a vent in the ceiling, as in cat.4, must lead into the open air, although this cannot have been possible in the 'kitchen-basement' shown in the picture exhibited here). The table is not a 'proper table,' in the sense in which Hogarth, or any other contemporary artist, would have used the term. He would have meant a specially constructed dais, such as the one shown in cat.4, rather than the assortment of crude wooden trestles shown here. Furthermore only one student is provided with an individual reflector-lamp, although, as one can see in cat.4, such lights would usually have been placed at regular intervals along the benches, for the use of all the students. Finally, although the benches are semi-circular they are wholly impractical, and provide no means of supporting the drawing-boards which rest uncomfortably on the artists' knees – unlike the circular benches shown in cat.4, which have sloping tops. If this really was the equipment which Hogarth inherited from Thornhill, it is difficult to understand why it was held in such special regard. A final – and more serious problem – is the artist's style. Several figures, such as the man at the extreme right, are superficially

Fig.1 Anon *A Life Class*, red chalk on paper
The Trustees of the British Museum

reminiscent of Hogarth and Hayman. And yet the figures at the far left are handled in a totally different manner. It would be difficult to find an 18th-century painter, either British or Continental, who painted in this hybrid manner. In the light of the above evidence, the authenticity of this work must be seriously open to question. It seems likely that it is rather a deliberately conceived fake, produced sometime during the 19th century.

How the picture entered the Royal Academy's collection is to be found in the Royal Academy Council Minutes of 1885. On 12 May it was recorded; 'Messrs Hogarth [sic], offering a picture by Hogarth of the members of the Academy, opened by him in Peter's Court, St. Martin's Lane studying from the Life Model for 100 guineas. To be asked to send for it for inspection' (R.A. Council Minutes, vol.8, p.245). On 26 May it was resolved by the Council to buy the painting (op. cit., vol.8, p.248). The British Museum has recently acquired a red-chalk drawing (1990-7-28-50) (fig.1), which is closely related in terms of composition to the picture exhibited here, although there are a number of significant alterations in the positioning of individual figures.

I am grateful to Robin Simon who first suggested that the present picture might be a fake, and to Dr. Brian Allen who also examined the painting after its conservation.   M.P.

A Life Class (? St. Martin's Lane Academy)   4
BRITISH SCHOOL

Oil on canvas, unfinished; 48.2 x 64.7 cm
c.1760

PROVENANCE: Presented by William Smith to the Royal Academy in 1871

EXHIBITED: Derby, 1934 (Wright bi-centenary); Sheffield, Graves Art Gallery, 1934; Royal Academy 1951 (1); Nottingham 1959 (52); Arts Council, 1961 (47); Tate Gallery 1982; Derby 1984 (92)

LITERATURE: Royal Academy, 1931, p.150, repr.

Royal Academy of Arts, London

In the late 19th century this picture was confused with *An Academy by Lamplight*, exhibited by Joseph Wright at the Society of Artists in 1769 (Yale Center for British Art) (see cat.38). As a result the picture has continually been attributed to that artist, despite the fact that stylistically it has nothing in common with any of Wright's works, and that, in its unfinished state, it would not have been exhibited publically. Nonetheless it is a picture of immense interest, and perhaps of considerable historical importance, as there is reason to believe that it may

be the only known depiction of the St. Martin's Lane Academy. Several factors support this hypothesis. In the first place, the relatively small room in which the artists are situated accords more closely with descriptions of the St. Martin's Lane Academy than the barn-like structure which has in the past been identified with St. Martin's Lane (for discussion of this point see cat.3). Secondly, the oil lamp is very similar to the one visible in Elias Martin's *Cast Room at the Royal Academy* (cat.6), where similar brackets secure the lamp to the ceiling and wall. Furthermore, one cast which appears on the shelf behind the artists (the second from the left) is also included in Zoffany's *Academicians of the Royal Academy* (at the extreme left on the back wall, see cat.5). The re-appearance of the lamp and the cast is significant as we know that in 1767 various pieces of equipment, including benches and casts, were taken from the St. Martin's Lane Academy to Dalton's warehouse, the prospective headquarters of what was shortly to become the Royal Academy (Whitley, 1928, vol.1, p.234). Finally, although it has not been possible to identify the artists seated prominently in the foreground, the features of the man second from the left bear a close resemblance to those of Johan Zoffany, who came to England in 1760. Admittedly this argument is speculative. Nevertheless, this picture seems much more likely to represent the so-called Second St. Martin's Lane Academy than cat.3, which is almost certainly a 19th century fake.   M.P.

The Academicians of the Royal Academy   5
JOHAN ZOFFANY   (COL PLATE II)
(Frankfurt am Main 1733-London 1810)

Oil on canvas; 100.7 x 147.3 cm
1771-72

PROVENANCE: Presumably painted for George III

EXHIBITED: Royal Academy, 1772 (290); British Institution, 1814 (163); British Institution, 1826 (158), 1827 (147); Royal Academy, 1934 (359), 1946 (50), 1951 (28); Queen's Gallery, 1968; Royal Academy, 1968 (12); Queen's Gallery, 1974 (34); National Portrait Gallery, 1977 (74); Royal Academy, 1986 (171); Cardiff, 1990 (59)

LITERATURE: Walpole, 1849, I, p.xviii, no.1; Leslie and Taylor, 1865, vol.1, pp.446-8; Manners and Williamson, 1920, pp.28-34, and p.211; Whitley, 1928, vol.1, p.271; Millar, 1969, no.1210; Kemp, 1975, pp.14-15, figs. 2-4; Hedley, 1975, pp.69, 73, 86, 94, 114; Webster, 1977, no.74; Penny, 1986, no.171; Evans, 1990, no.59

ENGRAVED: Mezzotint by Richard Earlom, 1773

Her Majesty the Queen

This painting shows the assembled Royal Academicians, together with two male models in the newly-founded Royal Academy of Arts. Although it is not the first painting of the members of a British artist's society – see Gawen Hamilton's *Conversation of Virtuosi* of 1735 (National Portrait Gallery), and cat.4 in this exhibition – it is the greatest. According to Horace Walpole, Zoffany made no design for the painting 'but clapped in the artists as they came to him, and yet all the attitudes are easy and natural, most of the likenesses strong ...' (Manners and Williamson, 1920, p.28). The grouping of the figures in the composition however, which reflects the various artists' standing within the existing status quo, suggests that Zoffany knew perfectly well where he felt everyone ought to be fitted in. The identity of all the sitters in the picture is known (see Manners and Williamson, 1920, p.28 for key). For the present it is sufficient to single out those who are most relevant to the themes studied in this exhibition. Seated in the foreground at the extreme left is the painter of this work, Johan Zoffany himself (cat.75). Standing at the back at the extreme left is Giovanni Cipriani (cat.49). Just in front of him, to the right is Benjamin West (cat.29). The figure seated with the drawing board, to the right of West's knee is Mason Chamberlin (cat.77). On Chamberlin's right, his hands resting on his knees, is Francis Hayman (cat.50). The figure dressed in black, to Hayman's right, holding the ear-trumpet, is Sir Joshua Reynolds, first President of the Royal Academy – and famously hard of hearing (cat.71). To Reynold's right, stroking his chin, and looking towards the model, is Dr. William Hunter, Professor of Anatomy (cats. 75 and 77). Richard Wilson leans against the right-hand side of the chimney-piece (cat.48), while the man putting the model's hand into a rope-loop is George Michael Moser, first Keeper of the Academy Schools (cat.46). The figure standing at the extreme right, with the cane, is Richard Cosway (cat.35), while behind him, and to his immediate left, is Joseph Nollekens (cats. 31 and 36).

The room depicted was in the Royal Palace at Old Somerset House on the Strand, where the Royal Academy had been given permission to run drawing classes from the life and from the Antique by George III (Hutchison, 1956, pp.7-8). The presence of the semi-circular benches, and the lamp, suggest that this was the room in which life drawing usually took place. The presence of the plaster écorché figure (cats.75 and 89) indicates perhaps that the room was used also for Hunter's lectures on anatomy. The centrality of life drawing to the curriculum of the newly-founded Academy is suggested not only by the presence of two male models, but the manner in which the focus of the sitters' attention is centred largely on them. Indeed, in his inaugural lecture at the Royal Academy, Sir Joshua Reynolds had not only stressed the importance of the living model but had confirmed that a 'variety of subjects' would be available to students (Reynolds, 1975, p.21). Two male models, of different ages are shown. The youth in the foreground undresses, while at the same time taking up a pose

reminiscent of the classical statue of the *Spinario* (Haskell and Penny, 1981, no.78). The older man, seated on the dais, raises his right arm, which is about to be held in position by the suspended rope Moser is about to place around his hand.

In January 1769 rules had been laid down concerning the running of the Life School, or 'Academy of Living Models.' Briefly, there were two terms each year; Summer and Winter. All life drawing was done in the evening, from six o'clock in Winter and from four o'clock in Summer. Male and female models were supplied. No unmarried man under the age of 20 was allowed to draw from the female model (Hutchison, 1968, pp.49 and 52). While it was never specified that the two female members of the Academy, Mary Moser and Angelica Kauffman, were forbidden to study from the model, their portraits on the wall in this work, rather than in the room itself, suggest that it would have been deemed improper for them to have done so (see also cat.34).   I.B./M.P.

Cast Room at the Royal Academy   6

ELIAS MARTIN   (COL PLATE III)
(Stockholm 1739-1818)

Oil on canvas; 122 x 98 cm
Signed and dated 1770

PROVENANCE: Bought 1910 at auction (A.B. Bukowski)

EXHIBITED: Royal Academy, 1770 (124); Stockholm 1950 (94); Stockholm 1985

LITERATURE: Graves 1905-6, p.201, no.124; Hoppé, 1933; Waterhouse, 1981, p.234

The Royal Academy of Fine Arts, Stockholm

Exhibited at the Royal Academy in 1770 as *A Picture of the Royal Plaister Academy*, this is the earliest known representation of the Cast Room of the Royal Academy of Arts. The casts depicted are, from left to right, Michelangelo's *Bacchus*, a group of two boys quarrelling over a game of knucklebones (also known as *The Cannibal*), *Mercury*, the *Callipygian Venus*, a wolf or hound, and *Meleager*. All the casts have been attenuated, which creates a greater sense of monumentality.

Elias Martin was born in Stockholm, and studied in Paris from 1766 to 1768 under Claude-Joseph Vernet. He came to England in 1768, and on 3 November 1769 was admitted as a student at the Royal Academy Schools (Hutchison, 1962, p.134). On 2 January 1769 the Academy had set out the 'Rules and Orders for the Plaister Academy.' They were as follows: 'There shall be Weekly, set out in the Great Room, One or more Plaister Figures by the Keeper, for the Students to draw after, and no Student shall presume to move the said Figures out of the Places where they have been set by the Keeper, without his leave first obtained for that Purpose. When any Student hath taken possession of a Place in the Plaister Academy, he shall not be removed out of it, till the Week in which he hath taken it is expired. The Plaister Academy, shall be open every Day (Sundays and Vacation times excepted) from Nine in the Morning till Three in the Afternoon' (Hutchison, 1968, p.49).

In 1770 Martin became one of the first Associate Royal Academicians and continued to work and exhibit in England until 1780 when he returned to Sweden. In 1781 he became a member of the Stockholm Academy. He returned to England briefly, between 1788 and 1791, although he subsequently went back to Sweden. The Royal Academy seems to have been unaware of his whereabouts in later life. In 1832 the Council resolved 'that a period of sixty years having elapsed since the election of Elias Martin Associate and no proof of his actual assistance having reached the Members of the Royal Academy for many years ... it be recommended to the General Assembly to erase the name of Elias Martin from the list of Associates' (Hutchison, 1968, pp.101-2).   M.P.

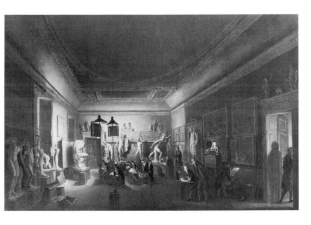

The Antique School of the Royal   7
Academy at New Somerset House   (COL PLATE IV)
BRITISH SCHOOL

Oil on canvas; 109.2 x 165.1 cm
c.1780-83

PROVENANCE: Presented by George IV to Lord Ashbrook of Old Windsor; at his sale purchased by W. Martin of Eton; bought by J. Thurwood at Cleave & Underhay's Sale Room, Windsor, where it remained until 1877; the Royal Academy purchased it from James Stewart in 1878.

EXHIBITED: Nottingham 1959 (53); Arts Council 1960 (48), Royal Academy 1963 (4); Hampstead Arts Centre 1966; Royal Academy 1968 (879); Arts Council 1972 (88); Tate 1982

LITERATURE: Manners and Williamson, 1920, pp.33-34

Royal Academy of Arts, London

There is no evidence to confirm the traditional attribution of this painting to Johan Zoffany. Manners and Williamson (1920, pp.33-34) identified the professor in the room as George Michael Moser, first Keeper to the Academy, although this remains speculative. The picture may well, however, be dated c.1780-83, namely between the removal of the Academy to New Somerset House and the appointment of Agostino Carlini in succession to Moser. Casts from the Antique are

illuminated by oil-lamps with large triple reflectors set up on high standards. Each student's easel is illuminated by its own oil-lamp and reflector. A lamp and reflector are also situated in front of the desk of the Keeper, strongly delineating his features. Casts include, from left to right: the *Dancing Faun*, the *Wrestlers, Belvedere Torso, Cincinnatus, Apollo Belvedere, Borghese Gladiator,* and *Meleager* (Haskell and Penny, 1981, nos. 8, 23, 34, 43, 60, 80 and 94). A screen has been inserted along the wall behind the *Belvedere Torso* to sharpen the contours. This practice appears to have been imported from Italy and was recommended to artists by English writers on art from the mid 17th century. Richard Symonds (1650-52, fo.75), a royalist who was in Rome in 1650-52, mentioned it in his *Secrete intorno La Pittura* (Beal, 1978; Talley, 1981, chap.10). Burney's *Antique Room, New Somerset House* (cat.39) shows the same room depicted from the opposite end.   I.B.

Apelles and Campaspe   8
Sir JOHN BAPTIST DE MEDINA
(Brussels 1659/60 - Edinburgh 1710)

Oil on canvas; 125.7 x 125.7 cm

PROVENANCE: By descent to the present owner

EXHIBITED: Scottish National Portrait Gallery 1989

LITERATURE: Waterhouse, 1981, p.237; Holloway, 1989, p.40, repr.

The Rt. Hon. the Earl of Wemyss and March, K.T.

The subject depicts the celebrated Greek painter Apelles painting Campaspe, mistress of Alexander the Great. According to Pliny, while Apelles was painting Campaspe, Cupid, who asssisted the artist by grinding his colours, ensured that the artist fell in love with her. Alexander, who admired Apelles' work, subsequently gave Campaspe to him. She became Apelles' mistress and the model for his most celebrated picture, *Aphrodite rising from the Sea*.

Although contemporary depictions of the artist and model in a private studio setting – as opposed to the Academy – were not common in the 17th or 18th centuries, the use of classsical episodes, as a form of allegory, were increasingly employed. Moreover, the academic model was traditionally associated with the male figure, but the studio model was more often linked with the female form. Indeed, even in classical times there had been no attempt to quantify the female form, which was regarded in a highly subjective manner. Commonly assumed to be the artist's mistress, the female model was looked on as a physical embodiment of his painterly muse. Although there are few British depictions of the present subject it was popular on the Continent from the late 17th century (see Cipriani in Boschloo et al ed.,1989, p.64 ff) to the early 19th century, when the subject was treated by Jacques Louis David in 1814 (Musée des Beaux Arts, Lille).

Sir John de Medina arrived in England in 1686, then moved to Edinburgh in 1693-4 where he painted numerous portraits of the Scottish nobility and gentry. *Apelles and Campaspe* is his only known historical composition, although he produced illustrations for a folio edition of Milton's *Paradise Lost* in 1688.   M.P.

Self-Portrait   (COL PLATE V) **9**
Sir GODFREY KNELLER
(Lubeck 1646 - London 1723)

Oil on canvas; 105 x 113.7 cm
c.1670

PROVENANCE: P. Peypers, Antwerp, 1903; Fievez sale, Brussels, 5.12.1906, lot 13; Ehrich Galleries, New York; American Art Galleries, sale George A. Hearn, Plaza Hotel, New York, 25.2.1918 cat.no. 413 as *Portrait of an artist* by F. Bol; R. Cook, Esq., London; Sotheby's, London, 19.11.1986, lot 33, as *Portrait of the artist* by G. Kneller.

EXHIBITED: The Hague 1903, *Exposition de Portraits Anciens*, no.26, as *Portrait d'un jeune homme* by F. Bol; Douwes 1981 as *Self-portrait of the artist as an engraver* by F. Bol

LITERATURE: Hofstede de Groot, 1903, no.26, as by F. Bol; de Kay 1919; Blanert, 1982, no.R63; Stewart, 1983, p.5, no.21a, and p.89, no.12A

Mrs A. Alfred Taubman

The painting, formerly attributed to Ferdinand Bol, is now ascribed to Kneller (Stewart, 1983, p.5, no.21a). Painted when the artist was in his mid-twenties, it shows a young man seated at a table covered with Dutch cloth, where objects associated with the artist's training are arranged. The knife and sharpened sticks, probably charcoal drawing sticks (Lambert, 1981, pp.14-15; idem, 1984, pp.30-32), show the sitter as a draughts-man, rather than an engraver as often described. The subject of the painting is the artist's training, and objects associated with his education gain significance from the fact that the sitter is a draughtsman. The objects on the table – the bust, the écorché figure, and the engraving of a female nude – refer to the three central aspects of academic education, namely the Antique, anatomy, and the study of the living model. The bust has been

described as *Seneca* (Blankert, 1982, p.169, no.R63). The écorché can be identified as the *Écorché posed as an archer* of which four bronze versions are known (Amerson, 1975, p.282, no.28; pp.282-85, no.29; and p.285, nos. 30 and 31). The écorché in Kneller's *Self-portrait* reverses the statuettes in the Musée Bonnat, Bayonne, and the Statens Museum, Copenhagen (Amerson, 1975, figs. 211 and 212), and is of the same type as the écorché attributed to Cigoli (see cat.90) on sale at Paul Brandt in Amsterdam (sale of Dr. Hugo Oelze's collection, 23-26 April 1968; see *The Connoisseur*, July 1968, p.285, ill.4). According to Amerson this type of écorché originated in 16th century Italy. The draughtsman is copying the engraving, which acts as a substitute for the living model (note the piece of paper on which the knife and charcoal sticks lie). Engravings were, of course, extremely important in art education. Moreover, from the beginning of the 17th century drawing books were published in most European countries including Holland (Bolten, 1985). These copy-books, or 'printed academies,' had the function of substitutes or complements to actual educational institutions (Bignamini, 1986-87, pp.436-38). They made a wide range of visual examples available to the artist. Although the female model depicted here is akin to Venus, her pose is ultimately derived from an antique-type of Apollo standing with one arm over his head (Bober and Rubinstein, 1986, no.35, the *Apollo Citharoedos*). The Uffizi *Apollino* (Haskell and Penny, 1981, no.7) is one of several replicas of this antique type derived from Praxiteles' lost original. Poses designed for ideal male models were often adapted to the female model and vice-versa, a practice which led Blake to produce his *Naked Youth* of c.1779-80 (cat.27).

Kneller's *Self-portrait* was probably painted in Amsterdam, where the artist trained under Ferdinand Bol. Subsequently, in 1672-75, Kneller visited Flanders and Italy. He settled in London in 1676, was Principal Painter to the King from 1688, and the first Governor of the Academy established in Great Queen Street, London, in 1711.

I am grateful to Monique Kornell for help in identifying the écorché figure in this work.   I.B.

The Artist, David Allan   **10**
DOMENICO CORVI (Viterbo 1721 - Rome 1803)

Oil on canvas; 74.3 x 61.3 cm
1774

PROVENANCE: Mrs. John Greig, New York; Presented to the Royal Scottish Academy, 1866; Presented to the Scottish National Portrait Gallery, 1910

EXHIBITED: Scottish Arts Council, 1973 (9)

LITERATURE: Crouther Gordon, 1951, p.27

Scottish National Portrait Gallery

Domenico Corvi was one of the leading history painters in Rome at the time that David Allan (b.1744-d.1796) was resident there, from 1768/69 to 1775 (see entry in DBVI). A member of the *Accademia di San Luca* from 1756, Corvi (see entry in DBI) was intermittently Director of the *Accademia del Nudo* in Campidoglio between 1757 and 1802. On 27 April 1773 Allan was awarded the first premium of the Concorso Balestra for his painting of *The Departure of Hector* (Galleria Nazionale di San Luca, Rome). Corvi himself had won the Concorso in 1750. In this portrait the artist is shown painting from a reduced cast of the *Borghese Gladiator* and is perhaps a token of respect to a foreign friend, who had spent time in Rome to perfect his education and who had been very successful at the Roman Academy. Allan's Italian works comprise lively scenes of contemporary life in Rome, (see for instance, the series of drawings in the Royal Collections). He also copied a number of Old Master paintings, including

Raphael's *Disputa* (Christie's, London, 14.11.1989, lot 71), some of which were commissioned by Scottish patrons (for instance, Guido Reni's *Aurora* and the *Aldobrandini Marriage* for Patrick Home in 1775). He is known to have studied antique figure painting (for example, his album *Memorandums & Sketches of the Ancient Pictures of Herculaneum* [sic], National Gallery of Scotland) and to have painted ancient sites such as the *Virgil's Tomb near Naples* of 1773 (National Gallery of Scotland). A version of this portrait was on sale at Sotheby's London, in 1981 (9.12.1981, lot 170). I.B.

Self-Portrait with Joseph Wilton and a student 11

JOHN HAMILTON MORTIMER
(Eastbourne 1740 - London 1779)

Oil on canvas; 76.2 x 63.5 cm
c.1765

PROVENANCE: Presented by T. Humphrey Ward, 1889

EXHIBITED: Royal Academy, 1890 (26); Royal Academy, 1934 (302); Arts Council, 1961 (23); Arts Council, 1962 (49); Royal Academy, 1963 (24); British Council, 1966 (34); Eastbourne and Kenwood, 1968 (3); Royal Academy, 1968 (25); British Council 1977

LITERATURE: Allen, 1984, pp.195-203; Sunderland, 1986, p.131, no.32

Royal Academy of Arts, London

The painting, formerly dated c.1778-79, has been redated to c.1765 by John Sunderland (1986, p.132) who has suggested that it recalls earlier times, when Mortimer and the sculptor Joseph Wilton (b.1722-1803) were associated with the Academy attached to the Duke of Richmond's Cast Gallery of 1758-62 (Bignamini 1988A, pp.450-52). This Gallery complemented the teaching offered by William Shipley's Drawing School, 1753-68, and the second St. Martin's Lane Academy, 1753-68. In 1758 Wilton was made Director of the Duke of Richmond's Academy and Giovanni Battista Cipriani (cat.49) was in charge of instruction in painting. Mortimer was

among the students. The three figures in Mortimer's painting are Wilton (supervising), Mortimer (drawing after the Antique), and a young student (holding an antique head). An anonymous copy consisting of two figures only (Mortimer and a young student) is preserved at the National Portrait Gallery (Sunderland, 1986, p.131, no.32a). I.B.

Sleeping Nymphs by a Fountain 12

Sir PETER LELY (COL PLATE VI)
(Soest, Westphalia, 1618 - London 1680)

Oil on canvas; 128.9 x 144.8 cm
Early 1650s

PROVENANCE: Bought in Paris by Charles Fairfax Murray; his gift, 1911

EXHIBITED: Royal Academy, 1960 (17); National Portrait Gallery, 1978 (25); Washington 1985 (20)

LITERATURE: Collins Baker, 1912, I, p.139 n.; Beckett, 1951, no.594; Sunderland, 1976, p.233; Millar, 1978, no.25; Murray, 1980, p.78, no.555; Rogers 1985, (20)

By permission of the Governors of Dulwich Picture Gallery

Collins Baker (1912, I, p.139 n.), who saw the painting in the collection of Charles Fairfax Murray, dated it prior to Lely's arrival in England in the late 1640s. The Dulwich catalogue of 1926 dated it to 1670. Sir Oliver Millar (1978, no.25) preferred a date in the early 1650s, when Lely is known to have painted similar subjects (see, for instance, *Cimon and Iphigenia*, Doddington Hall, Lincs; exh. *Treasured Possessions*, Sotheby's, London, Dec. 1983 – Jan. 1984). Millar has drawn attention to the influence of Van Dyck's paintings such as *Cupid and Psyche* (Royal Collection; Millar 1982, no.58), which was in Lely's collection in 1660 (Larsen, 1988, II, no.1043). Malcolm Rogers (1985, no.20) suggested that the sleeping nymph at the back echoes in reverse the sleeping Ariadne in Titian's *Andrians* (Prado, Madrid) possibly known by Lely in the reverse engraving by G.A. Podesta. Other sources may be mentioned. A nymph sleeping by a fountain or spring is a figure found in classical sculpture. The nymph to the left in Lely's painting is

reminiscent of a Roman statue of the 2nd century A.D. (Bober and Rubinstein, 1986, no.62), while the nymph to the right resembles the sleeping *Hermaphrodite* (Haskell and Penny, 1981, no.48; Bober and Rubinstein, 1986, no.98), a type particulary influential in the 17th century and well known to Flemish artists like Rubens and English virtuosi like John Evelyn, who purchased a small ivory copy by François Duquesnoy while in Rome in the late 1640s. Many elements converge in Lely's painting: the Antique, Old Masters, and the study of the living model. Millar (1978, p.11, fig.3) and Rogers (1985, p.83, fig.1) have ascribed to Lely the drawing of a *Female nude reclining, seen from the back* formerly in the collection of C.R. Rudolf (sold Sotheby's, Amsterdam, 18.4.1977, lot 40). Yet, the same drawing has been related recently to Subleyras's *Étude académique de femme nue vue de dos* of c.1739 (Galleria Nazionale d'Arte Antica, Palazzo Barberini, Rome; Paris and Rome, 1987, no.59). Until a complete catalogue of Lely's work (especially the drawings) and a study of the artist's collection are produced no firm conclusion can be drawn. One general remark, however, can be made: paintings such as *Sleeping Nymphs* testify to Lely's use of the nude female model in his studio. Moreover, written documents and visual evidence suggest that Lely supervised drawings after the living model, both male and female, executed by students who attended the Academy of c.1673.

I.B.

Male nude seated 13

? BRITISH SCHOOL

Oil on canvas; 65.3 x 51.7 cm
? 1750s

Private Collection

There is no provenance known for this painting apart from the fact that it was bought privately in London a few years ago. It is an 'academy,' that is a pictorial representation of the male nude model as he posed before students and artists at academies of art. The 'academy' developed as a pictorial *genre* from nudes in the context of historical compositions, from representations of nude models in paintings of life classes at work (cat. nos. 4, 5, 7) and from life drawings themselves. As far as is known, the 'academy' of the 18th century is associated with the *envoi*, which *pensionnaires* of the French Academy in Rome were required to execute. An early example is Jean Bernard Restout's *Morpheus* of the late 1750s (Rubin, 1977, pp.88-89). The French 'academy' developed fully between the late 1770s and early 1780s, when Jacques-Louis David painted his *Académie*

d'homme, dite 'Hector' and *Académie d'homme, dite 'Patrocle'* (Paris, 1989, nos. 30 and 37). No English 'academy' of the same period has so far come to light except for this painting. The use of red in the rendering of the flesh (face, shoulder and legs) and the handling of the brush would suggest an artist in the circle of Francis Hayman. The uneasy handling of anatomy suggests the hand of a student, possibly one who attended the second St. Martin's Lane Academy in the 1750s.

I.B.

Male nude, with hands bound 14

WILLIAM ETTY (York 1787-1849)

Oil on millboard; 59.7 x 43.2 cm
c.1828-30

PROVENANCE: Sir Claude Phillips Bequest 1924

EXHIBITED: York, 1948 (23); Arts Council, 1955 (17), repr. p. IIIa; Usher Gallery, Lincoln, 1975 (35); Musée des Beaux Arts, Dijon, 1979 (9)

LITERATURE: Farr, 1958, cat.234; Woodward, 1962, p.121 repr.; York, 1963, vol.2, p.39

York City Art Gallery

This work, which is one of Etty's most dramatic oil studies of the male nude, probably dates from the late 1820s. By this time Etty, then in his early forties, was regarded as something of a phenomenon in his continual attention to the model in the Life Class. In 1831 Constable, who was himself Visitor in the Life Class at the Royal Academy, noted: 'Sass – the inexorable Sass – and the imperturbable Etty are never absent; they set an excellent example to the Modles [sic] for regularity.' But he added acidly, 'I presume not to hold them up as examples in any other respect.' (quoted in Farr, 1958, p.56). This study forms an interesting comparison with cat.15, not only in terms of its dramatic pose, but in the comparative coolness of the flesh tones, a fact which suggests that it may not have been made in the Academy, under the intense light of a large oil lamp, but in the artist's own studio (see cat.1). The model, in its highly theatrical posture, does not conform to the standard

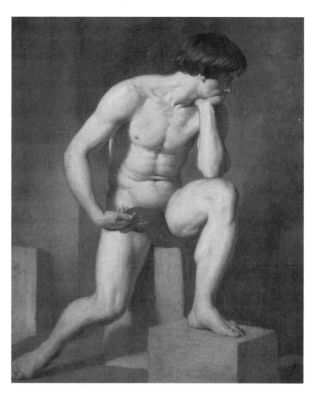

of objectivity usually demanded by academic strictures, but relies rather on a type of quasi-eroticism which ultimately derives from Caravaggio.   M.P

Male nude, seated   (COL PLATE VII) **15**
WILLIAM ETTY (York 1781-1849)

Oil on board; 61.4 x 50.2 cm
c.1815-18

PROVENANCE: Robert Frank Ltd; Christie's 22.11.1985, lot 90

Private Collection

This is among the most severely 'academic' of Etty's life studies. Painted in oil – a medium which Fuseli had encouraged him to use – and on millboard, it exemplifies the type of finished life-study which Etty was capable of producing during the evening Life Class at the Royal Academy Schools. Etty's method of painting from the life, an activity which spanned three separate evenings, can be summarised as follows: on the first evening he drew the figure either in chalk or in charcoal on an unprepared piece of millboard. Having done this he carefully inked in the outline of the figure. Afterwards, at home, he rubbed size into the board to prepare the surface for oil paint. On the second evening he began to work in oils, concentrating on the figure only, ensuring that it remained in sharp relief from the background. On the third evening the study was completed by the addition of a glaze, into which local colour was worked rapidly (Gilchrist, 1855, vol.1, pp.5-8). A first-hand account of the practice in painting in oils from the life during successive evenings may be found in David Wilkie's diary entries over the summer of 1808, (see Cunningham, 1843, vol.1, pp.183 ff).

Many of Etty's life-studies survive. In May 1850, after his death, Christie's sold off more than 800 of them from the artist's studio. At the time *The Athenaeum* (11 May 1850) objected to the sale, which it said was 'likely to be as pernicious to art as to morals', because in addition to 'putting into the possession of any casual person works whose purer aim and

intention might be mistaken', the flooding of the market with so many similar works would engender plagiarisms. In the event the *Art Journal* (1850, vol.12, p.199) stated that many of the studies were bought up by artists, although it added that the principal danger was that they would be worked up and sold as finished pictures. In 1860 Richard and Samuel Redgrave confirmed this prediction, noting that 'it is to be regretted that few remain in an entirely genuine state – many have been altered and completed *pictorially* for the dealers, by painters who lent themselves to such a practice (Redgrave, 1947, p.284). Many of Etty's studies, especially those of females, show signs of having been 'improved' and historicised by the addition of garlands of flowers, leafy glades, and streams. This study, by way of contrast, is very straightforward, and seems not to have been tampered with, save perhaps for the addition of a wisp of red drapery which conceals the genitalia. It probably dates from the late teens and exhibits a high degree of finish, especially around the hands and feet, indicating that it might have been worked up specially by the artist to demonstrate his virtuosity.   M.P.

Male nude, standing, with a staff   **16**
JOHN CONSTABLE
(East Bergholt 1776 - London 1837)

Oil on canvas; 60.5 x 50 cm
c.1808-10

PROVENANCE: By descent to the present owner

EXHIBITED: Colchester 1950; New York 1989

LITERATURE: Shirley, 1933, p.219; Fleming-Williams, 1975, pp.313-15; New York 1989, p.13, repr.

Private Collection

Aside from William Etty, the only other British artist who left a significant number of oil studies from the living model is John Constable, by whom at least nine such works are known. John Constable began to work from the life at the Royal Academy in 1800 (see cat.26), although the majority of his oil studies from the model have generally been ascribed to the period of the

Male nude, reclining (COL PLATE VIII) 17

JOHN CONSTABLE
(East Bergholt 1776 - London 1837)

Oil on canvas; 48 x 60 cm
? c.1808-10

PROVENANCE: By descent to the present owner

EXHIBITED: Colchester, 1950; Christchurch Mansion, Ipswich 1955

LITERATURE: Shirley, 1933, 219, repr.; Constable 1975, p.119, repr.; Hoozee, 1979, no.541, repr.

Private Collection

This painting has been tentatively ascribed to William Etty (see Shirley, 1933, p.219), principally because Etty is known to have presented Constable with one of his own oil studies in 1836 (Gilchrist, 1855, vol.2, pp.59-60), and that, as this study differs from other known life studies by Constable in terms of the model's pose and the relationship of the figure to its setting, it may therefore be the picture in question. There is not, however, any reason to hold that the painting is not by Constable. In the first place, the cool tonality differs from that found in the majority of Etty's life-studies. Secondly, and more significantly, the study relates in terms of its treatment of light and shade, the modelling of the flesh, and the relation of the figure to the ground, to several chalk drawings by Constable of the male nude, including one of a reclining male figure (fig.2), which has been dated to around 1808 (Shirley, 1933, pp.216-7). M.P.

Fig.2 JOHN CONSTABLE *Reclining male nude*
black chalk on paper, c.1807-8. Private Collection

early 1830s when he acted as a Visitor in the Life Schools (but see Parris et. al., 1976, no.84). There is good reason to believe that Constable was regularly making oil studies from the model as early as 1808. On July 14 of that year Wilkie recorded in his diary going to the Royal Academy, 'where I found the living figure sitting, and Robertson, Constable, and others, painting from her' (quoted by Fleming-Williams, 1975, p.314). During that summer and autumn Wilkie went regularly in the evenings to paint from the model, recording Constable's presence, and indeed accompanying him there on several occasions (op. cit., p.314-5). This study may well date from this period, especially given that the attitude of the figure, holding a staff, is far more conventional than the poses which Constable himself set when he was appointed a Visitor to the Academy's Life School in later life.

Constable was made a Visitor to the Life Class at the Royal Academy for the first time in January 1831, again in 1832, and for a third time just before his death in 1837. During his first Visitorship he set the models in a variety of poses based on old-master paintings, including a grouping of two male models based on Michaelangelo's *Last Judgement,* and a female model as *Eve,* apparently borrowed from Raphael's representation of Eve in the ceiling of the *Stanza della Segnatura* (see Beckett, III, p.35 ff). He wrote to C.R. Leslie at the time: 'I am quite popular in "the life", at all events I spare neither pains nor expense to become a good Academician. It cost me ten shillings for my *Garden of Eden* beside my own men being twice stopped on Sunday evening by the police ... thinking (as was the case) they had robbed some gentleman's garden' (Leslie, 1937, p.257). Constable himself produced an oil study of his re-creation of Eden, although it was destroyed (except for Eve's head) after the artist's death. An oil study of a female model, which is similar in style to this work, and may indeed date from the same period, was sold at Sotheby's in 1979 (18 July, lot 31). M.P.

II The Antique

The drawings, paintings and engravings selected for this section demonstrate the key role of classical statuary in the study of the figure by British artists during the 18th, and early 19th centuries. Among the exhibits are important examples of classical male statuary – the *Apollo Belvedere*, the *Farnese Hercules*, the *Belvedere Torso*, and the *Wrestlers* – including a drawing by Mulready (cat.20) whose inscription makes the point that an ability to draw from the Antique was required before students could advance to the living model. The central paradigm for the study of the female figure was the *Venus de Medici*. For this reason drawings of female classical statuary in this section are centred on this statue. The inclusion of Blake's *Naked Youth* (cat.27) among studies of the female body is designed to highlight the way in which the artist combines male and female attributes to create an androgynous figure which undermines the orthodox academic attitudes then being promoted by the Academy. Finally, the inclusion of Archer's painting of the *Elgin Marbles* (cat.41) and Haydon's *Lapith* from the Parthenon (25) serve to illustrate the point, which is taken up in subsequent sections, that the study of the Parthenon sculptures transformed not only artists' notions of classical statuary, but profoundly affected the way in which they viewed the living model.

Colour Plate X   WILLIAM MULREADY *The Wrestlers*, c.1801
The Board of Trustees, Victoria and Albert Museum, London (cat.20)

Belvedere Torso   (COL PLATE IX)   **18**

J.M.W. TURNER (London 1775-1851)

Black and red chalk, heightened with white, on brown paper;
61 x 50.8 cm
Signed: *Wm Turner*
Mid-1790s

PROVENANCE: Purchased in 1884 with 6 other academic
studies by the artist

The Board of Trustees, Victoria and Albert Museum,
London

This drawing of the *Belvedere Torso*, executed in red chalk, is
rather more sophisticated in its handling, and grasp of three-
dimensional form, than the study in black and white chalks of
the same statue in the Turner Bequest, which has been dated
to between 1789 and 1793 (TB V/D). Unlike the majority
of classical statues unearthed in Italy during the Renaissance
the *Torso* was left unrestored, perhaps on the advice of
Michelangelo, who apparently expressed a particular
admiration for this work (Haskell and Penny, 1981, no.80,
p.312). By the early 18th century small-scale replicas of the
Torso were common in London cast-shops (op. cit., p.313).
Nollekens presented a copy of the *Torso* to the Royal Academy,
while in 1842 Turner repeated the gesture (Gage, 1987, p.33).
See also cats. 28 and 34.   M.P.

Rear view of the *Dancing Faun*   **19**

Sir DAVID WILKIE (Cults, Fifeshire 1755 - Gibraltar 1841)

Black chalk, heightened with white, on paper; 49 x 30.8 cm
Inscribed, possibly by Wilkie: *D. Wilkie for admission to the
Antique Academy*
1805

PROVENANCE: Purchased 1966

EXHIBITED: St. Andrews and Aberdeen, 1985

LITERATURE: Campbell, 1969, p.398, fig.1; Campbell, 1979, I,
pp.43-4; St. Andrews 1985, cat.1

The National Galleries of Scotland, Edinburgh

This drawing has traditionally been thought to have been
drawn by Wilkie in 1799, to gain entry to the Trustees
Academy in Edinburgh. It seems more plausible, however, to
argue that it was the drawing with which the artist gained
entry to the Antique Academy at the Royal Academy Schools
in December 1805. Regarding his attempt to enter the Trustees
Academy Allan Cunningham noted how, despite a letter from
the Earl of Leven to the Secretary George Thomson, 'his
[Wilkie's] drawings failed to satisfy the eye of that gentleman;
he looked at the drawings of the modest and timid boy,
reperused the Earl's letter, shook his head, and finally refused to
admit him' (Cunningham, 1843, vol.1, pp.32-33). It was only
through Leven's personal appeal that Wilkie was eventually
admitted, and the artist later confessed to Cunningham, 'I, for
one, can allow no ill to be said of patronage; patronage made
me what I am, for it is plain that merit had no hand in my
admission' (loc. cit.). John Burnet described Wilkie's
attendance at the Trustees Academy: 'When Wilkie came to
our class he had much enthusiasm of a queer and silent kind,
and very little knowledge of drawing: he had made drawings, it

is true, from living nature in that wide academy of the world, and chiefly from men or boys, such groups as chance threw his way; but in that sort of drawing on which taste and knowledge are desired, he was far behind the others who, without a tithe of his talent, stood in the same class ... It was not enough for him to say "draw that antique foot, or draw this antique hand"; no, he required to know to what statue the foot or hand belonged; what was the action, and what the sentiment. He soon felt that in the true antique the action and sentiment pervade it from the crown of the head to the sole of the foot, and that unless this was known the fragment was not understood, and no right drawing of it could be made' (op. cit., vol.1, p.39). In May 1805 Wilkie went to London, and in July entered the Royal Academy Schools as a probationer. According to Cunningham Wilkie's probation was secured by a drawing of *Niobe* (op. cit., vol.1, p.74). This was perhaps the same red chalk drawing of the head *Niobe* which Wilkie had made at the Trustees Academy (ibid., p.40). On 15 July 1805 Wilkie wrote to a friend in Scotland: 'I am admitted as a probationer into the Royal Academy, which I attend from 11 till 2 o'clock, and from 5 till 7' (ibid., p.79). In December 1805 Wilkie was enrolled as a student at the Royal Academy Schools. This drawing, it is suggested, secured his admission. A cast of the *Dancing Faun* (Haskell & Penny, 1981, cat.34) is clearly shown at the left hand side of *The Antique Room of the Royal Academy at New Somerset House* (cat.7). M.P.

(University Art Gallery, Nottingham only)

The Wrestlers (COL PLATE X) 20
WILLIAM MULREADY
(Co. Clare, Ireland 1786 - London 1863)
Black and white chalks on green-grey paper; 36 x 33 cm
Inscribed: *for permission to draw from the living model W*^m *Mulready*
c.1801

PROVENANCE: Purchased at the artist's sale, Christie's, 28-30.4.1864, lot 237

EXHIBITED: South Kensington Museum, 1864 (no.115)

LITERATURE: Rorimer, 1972, cat.36, repr.; Heleniak 1980, p.7, repr.

The Board of Trustees, Victoria and Albert Museum, London

In May 1799 Mulready's parents asked the Royal Academician Thomas Banks to inspect a drawing of the cast of the *Apollo*, with a view to gaining entry for their son to the Royal Academy Schools. Although Banks did not apparently think Mulready's first effort was up to the required standard, he agreed to assist him on the strength of a second drawing presented to him a month later (see Heleniak, 1980, p.6). For six weeks Mulready attended a drawing school in Furnival's Inn, Holborn, after which he drew from the cast in Banks's studio. He·was admitted as a probationer to the Royal Academy in June 1800, and was admitted to the Royal Academy Schools on 23 October 1800. Heleniak states (op. cit., p.229, no.26) that it is not clear whether the date of Mulready's admission, cited here, was to the Antique Academy or to the Life Schools. Admission to the Schools usually meant that the student was permitted to enter the Antique Academy rather than the Life Schools, for which one had to serve a further apprenticeship. Given Mulready's age, however (he was 14), he was almost certainly admitted to the Antique Academy in October 1800. As Turner spent three years in the Antique Academy, (see cat.28), Mulready's drawing made, as the inscription says, to enable him to draw from the living model, may have not been executed until at least 1801.

A comparison with Bonington's student drawing of the *Wrestlers*, although executed some twenty years later, is revealing in the way that it highlights the difference in styles between English and French drawing techniques in the early 19th century. At the Academy Schools Mulready employs a comparatively broad hatching technique to describe the contours of the muscles, whereas Bonington, at the *École des Beaux Arts*, uses the stump in order to blend individual chalk marks, while at the same time emphasising the outline of the figures against a plain ground. M.P.

The Wrestlers 21
RICHARD PARKES BONINGTON
(Nottingham 1802 - Paris 1828)
Black chalk and stump, on paper; 40 x 53.3 cm
c.1820

PROVENANCE: Mrs R. Bonington sale, Sotheby's, 10.2.1838 (part of lot 4); M. Duncan, Liverpool, 1895; Purchased by Nottingham Corporation, 0. Byrne sale, Christie's 3 April 1962 (54)

EXHIBITED: Castle Museum, Nottingham, 1965; Prinz Max Palais, Karlsruhe, Germany, 1989-90

LITERATURE: Spencer, 1964, no.8; Cormack, 1989, p.24, repr.; Walker 1989, p.168

Nottingham Castle Museum and Art Gallery

The present study of *The Wrestlers* was apparently included as part of a lot of nine 'Academical Studies, pencil' sold upon the death of the artist's mother in 1838. A second study of the *Borghese Gladiator*, from the same sale, also belongs to the Castle Museum, Nottingham. Bonington's family moved to Calais in 1817, where he met Francois Louis Thomas Francia (1773-1839), who gave him lessons in watercolour. Shortly afterwards, towards the end of 1818, he migrated to Paris where he was introduced to Eugene Delacroix (1798-1863). Bonington entered the atelier of Antoine-Jean Gros (1771-1835) in April 1819, at the *École des Beaux Arts*, where daily drawing from the cast and the living model was an essential part of the curriculum (Boime, 1971, p.8). Bonington's

Wrestlers was almost certainly done in Gros's atélier, for although it is not inscribed, another of Bonington's cast drawings, of *Hercules*, is signed 'Bonington Eleve de M. Gros' (Cormack, 1989, p.24), as is a similar drawing of the *Marble Faun*, acquired in 1989 by the British Museum (1989-5-30-1). In France, far more than in England, the importance of 'finish' was stressed (see also cat.52), and although by this time David was living in exile, his ideas were still promulgated by pupils such as Gros. As a professor at the *École des Beaux Arts*, Gros stressed the primacy of drawing. Indeed the *Library of Fine Arts* noted that Bonington, even after leaving Gros, continued to work at the *École des Beaux Arts* in order to improve his ability to draw the figure (Shirley, 1940, p.16). According to James Roberts, an English artist who studied at the same time under Gros, Bonington asked permission to paint from the model, but was refused (see Dubuisson, 1924, p.34). He did however draw from the female model with Delacroix in private (op. cit., p.32, repr.).   M.P.

Apollo Belvedere   22

GILES HUSSEY (Dorset 1710-1788)

Pen and ink on paper; 53.4 x 38.1 cm
Inscribed in ink, at a later date, over an original inscription:
Dall' Hussey / drawn through a machine to take / the exact proportion
c.1730-37

PROVENANCE: Richardson; Lord Gainsborough; bought at his sale, 22.7.1953 by A.P. Oppé; by descent to the present owner

Private Collection

Giles Hussey was in Italy between 1730 and 1737 (see also cat.44). Although comparatively little of his work exists on which to found a fair assessment of his abilities, Hussey was evidently a very capable draughtsman. Seventy-two of his drawings were sold at Christie's on 1 May 1787, including lot 65: 'Two, *Hercules* and *Apollo*, from the antique.' This drawing may be the one referred to. Hussey studied in Naples, Bologna, and Rome, where we may assume he made this drawing of the *Apollo Belvedere*, with the aid of a camera obscura. In the earliest Renaissance drawings of the *Apollo Belvedere* the left forearm and part of the right hand are missing, but in 1532 or 1533 Montorsoli effected repairs to the statue – although these additions have now been removed (see Haskell and Penny, 1981, no.8). In Hussey's drawing three of the fingers on the right hand, and the thumb, are missing, indicating, perhaps, that Montorsoli's additions had became detached, or that the cast from which he drew – if such was the case – was damaged.

Hussey's use of the camera obscura here may well relate to his systematic study of the proportional defects of classical statuary. In 1745, in a conversation with George Vertue he revealed that: 'he found and discovered the Antient grecian Sculptors had no *Rule* or certain regular proportions for humane statue, parts, nor the whole-statue, this he said he discovered at Rome and demonstrated as a fact ... The Antique statue of *Herculus* [sic] – he said – faulty. The *Venus of Medicis* - also the *Appollo* [sic] – the *Laocoon* and his two sons, and the *Gladiator* tho' the most perfect statue of all, yet he thinks faulty, in proportions and in the possition [sic], and muscles' (Vertue, III, pp.127-8).   M.P.

Farnese Hercules   23

RICHARD DALTON (c.1715-1791)

Red chalk on paper; 75 x 53.3 cm
Inscribed: *R. Dalton F. 1742* and on the rock,
ΓΛΥΚΩΝ ΑΘΗΝΑΙΟΟ ΕΠΟΙΕΙ

PROVENANCE: Richardson; Lord Gainsborough; Sotheby's,
22.7.1922 (2445); by descent to the present owner

LITERATURE: Oppé, 1950 no.163

Private Collection

This meticulous red-chalk study relates to 13 drawings by
Dalton in the collection of Her Majesty the Queen, including a
second depiction of the *Farnese Hercules* by the artist (Oppé,
1950, 38-39). The origin of the drawings is related in a letter
dated 2 May 1741 by Lady Pomfret to Lady Hertford: 'This
morning Mr Dalton came, as he had promised and brought
some statues drawn in red chalk, that he said were for Lord
Brooke, and some copies from the little Farnese that he told me
were for your Ladyship. There is a very visible improvement
from the first of his drawings to those last finished, which indeed
were as good as any I have seen of the modern artists ... I am
endeavouring to get him leave to copy some things out of the
Capitol, an access to which is at present somewhat difficult'
(Pomfret, 1805, vol.3, pp.111-2). Clearly Dalton's drawings
were commissioned in the same spirit as Pompeo Batoni's 'paper
museum' of red-chalk drawings after the Antique, which were
done for Richard Topham 1671-1830) between 1727 and 1730
(Macandrew, 1978, pp. 131-50).

Some of the drawings, including this example, are dated to
1741, others to 1742. Among the other statues represented by
Dalton in the series are the *Borghese Warrior*, the *Apollo
Belvedere*, the *Venus de Medici*, and – the only non-classical
example – Bernini's *Apollo and Daphne* (Borghese Gallery).

Eight of Dalton's drawings were published in 1770 by John
Boydell as part of *A Collection of Twenty Antique Statues Drawn
after the Originals in Italy by Richard Dalton Esq*. The *Farnese
Hercules* was engraved as the seventh plate in the book, with
the following inscription: 'Hercules a labore quiescans in
Aedibus Farnesianis / To Chichester Fortesque Esqr This plate
is humbly inscrib'd by his most obedient serv. R. Dalton.' Most
of the plates in the book carried dedications; the *Apollo
Belvedere* is, for example, dedicated to Richard Mead, while the
Wrestlers (the drawing of which is lost) is dedicated to
Lord Bute.

At the time of Dalton's drawing the *Farnese Hercules* was in
its unrestored state in the Palazzo Farnese. A cast of the figure
also existed in the French Academy in Rome. At that time not
only were the extremities of the fingers missing on the left hand,
but its legs were substitutes which had been made by Guglielmo
della Porta on the advice of Michelangelo. In 1787, however
the statue's original legs were put back into place and the figure
restored. It was subsequently sent to Naples (Haskell and
Penny, 1981, cat.46). And yet, as Lady Pomfret's letter
indicates – and a comparison of Dalton's drawing with the
original confirms – the artist had almost certainly based his
study on a reduced copy of the statue, of which there were
numerous versions in plaster and bronze by the early 18th
century (see Haskell and Penny, 1981, p.232).   M.P.

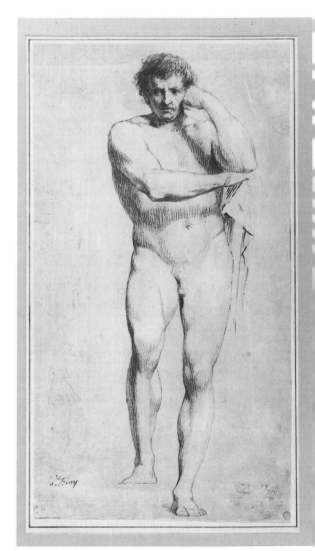

Male nude, in the attitude of Hercules (see cat.24)

Male nude, in the attitude of Hercules　　24

JAMES BARRY (Cork 1741 - London 1806)

Pen and ink and black chalk on brown paper; 35.5 x 21.4 cm
(including 1.5 cm strip added along the top).
Annotated in pen, lower left: *A. Barry*, and in ink at
lower right: *C. Bently*
c.1777-80

PROVENANCE: Earl of Warwick (Lugt 2600)

EXHIBITED: Hatton Gallery, Newcastle upon Tyne, 1974
(118); Courtauld Institute Galleries, London, 1975 (75)

LITERATURE: Pressly 1981, cat.80, p.257

Ralph Holland

This life drawing is a study for the statue of Hercules which
appears in the *Crowning of the Victors at Olympia*, one of six
murals which Barry painted for the Great Room at the Society
of Arts between 1777 and 1784. The figure of Hercules, who
treads on envy in the form of a serpent, is located at the extreme
left of the painting, and is matched by a statue of the goddess
Minerva on the right. The principle paradox in the context of
this exhibition is that Barry has used the living model as a basis
for an antique statue of Hercules, whereas the majority of works
on display demonstrate how classical statuary formed the basis
of life drawing within academic circles. It is, perhaps no
accident that Barry, in a conscious decision to rely on his own
creative drive, chose to take as his model a figure based on a life
drawing rather than the *Farnese Hercules*, which would have
been the obvious model.

In 1775, Barry, in *An Inquiry into the Real and Imaginary
Obstructions to the Acquisition of the Arts in England*, expressed
the need to defend the representation of nudity in classical
statuary: 'The Greek statues of the *Laocoon, Apollo, Meleager*, of
the *Belvedere, Hercules*, the *Fighting Gladiator*, and the *Venus de
Medici*, though altogether naked, yet surely there is nothing
in them offensive to modesty...' (Barry, 1809, vol.2, p.259). M.P.

Lapith from the Elgin Marbles　　25
(South metope XXVII)

BENJAMIN ROBERT HAYDON
(Plymouth 1786 - London 1846)

Black chalk on white paper; 73.3 x 54.5 cm
Inscribed: *1809 Sketched in Park Lane / In the Court yard now built
over (Duke of Gloucester) / then Lord Elgin – who bought the House of
Lady Cholomondely*

PROVENANCE: Purchased in 1881 from F.W. Haydon

The Trustees of the British Museum, London

The Elgin Marbles were first shown to the selected members of
the British public from the summer of 1807 in a shed which was
constructed specially by Lord Elgin behind a property in Park
Lane. Among the artists who came to inspect them there were
West, Lawrence, Wilkie, Fuseli, and Flaxman. The artist upon
whom they undoubtedly had the greatest impact, however, was
Benjamin Robert Haydon, whose diaries at the time are filled
with encomiums about every aspect of them. 'I felt,' he later
recalled, 'as if a divine truth had blazed inwardly upon my mind,
and I knew that they would at last rouse the art of Europe from
its slumber of darkness' (Elwin, 1950, p.78). According to
Haydon, the essential difference between the figures from the
Elgin Marbles and the Roman copies of Greek statues which
currently acted as paradigms, was that the Marbles exhibited
'the most heroic style of art combined with all the essential
details of actual life' (op. cit., p.77). Thus, they confirmed his
belief that the artist's primary duty was to study the human form
through life-drawing and the study of anatomy – as he believed
the sculptors of the Elgin Marbles had done.

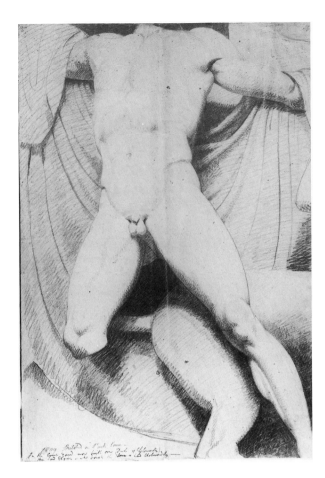

Haydon continued to draw from the Marbles, at fever pitch,
throughout 1808. Later he pasted many of them into enormous
scrapbooks which were intended as model-books for the
students who attended his 'School' from around 1815. This
drawing is taken from one of these scrapbooks, which are now
in the British Museum. Haydon, who attempted as far as
possible to match the scale of the Marbles with his own
drawings, later encouraged his pupils, including the Landseer
brothers and William Bewick, to do the same. Indeed, in
Haydon's system of education, the drawing from these antique
statues and reliefs was the climax of a student's training rather
than the beginning. In 1817 Haydon sent his pupils to the
Temporary Elgin Room at the British Museum, where the
Marbles were then housed: 'The astonishment of the people was
extraordinary; they would not believe they were Englishmen;
they continually asked if they were Italians. Their cartoons
(drawn the full size) of the *Fates*, the *Theseus* and the *Illissus*
literally made a noise in Europe' (Elwin, 1950, p.311).　　M.P.

introduction to Joseph Wilton, who was then Keeper of the Royal Academy Schools. The same day Constable wrote to his friend John Dunthorne: 'I am this morning admitted a student at the Royal Academy; the figure which I drew for admittance was the Torso' (Leslie, 1937, p.12; and Beckett, II, p.22). On 4 December 1799 Joseph Farington listed Constable as among those probationers who had qualified to be students at the Academy (Farington, IV, p.1317). Shortly afterwards, on 19 February 1800, Constable was enrolled in the Life Schools, although he did not receive his ticket, which gave him official permission to work from the living model, until 21 June that year. On the basis of the paucity of drawings by him from classical statuary, it has been argued that Constable spent very little time drawing from the Antique. Leslie noted: 'I have seen no studies made by Constable at the Academy from the antique, but many chalk drawings and oil paintings from the living model, all of which have great breadth of light and shade, though they are sometimes defective in outline' (Leslie, 1937, p.13). Graham Reynolds pointed out (Reynolds, 1973, p.40) that this drawing, which shows a lack of confidence in the handling of line, conforms with Leslie's description.   M.P.

Naked youth, seen from the side 27

WILLIAM BLAKE (London 1757-1827)

Black chalk 47.9 x 37 cm
Stamped 'J.D.F.' in oval
c.1779-80

PROVENANCE: Given by John Deffett Francis to the British Museum, April 1878

EXHIBITED: Detroit and Philadelphia, 1968 (92); Arts Council, 1972 (506), pl.91; Tate 1978 (8)

LITERATURE: Gilchrist, 1880, II, no.38; Binyon, 1898-1907, I, p.128, no.41; Keynes, 1927, no.3; Keynes, 1949, p.7, pl.1; Blunt, 1959, p.4; Bindman, 1977, pp.19-20, pl.8; Paley, 1978, p.20; Bindman, 1982, no.8

The Trustees of the British Museum, London

Male nude, in attitude of 26
Michelangelo's *Jonah* (COL PLATE XI)

JOHN CONSTABLE
(East Bergholt 1776 - London 1837)

Charcoal with black and white chalks on grey paper; 51.8 x 36 cm
Inscribed on the back in ink: *Drawn by my Father John Constable R.A., C.G. Constable*
c.1800-01

PROVENANCE: Presented by Rev. R.C. Lathom Browne

LITERATURE: Shirley 1933, p.215, no.1; Reynolds, 1973, cat.20, pl.9; Rosenthal, 1983, p.23 repr.

The Board of Trustees, Victoria and Albert Museum, London

One of four life drawings by Constable in the collection of the Victoria and Albert Museum. This work demonstrates the manner in which living models were posed at the Royal Academy to resemble figures taken from the Old Masters, as well as from antique statuary. Here the male model takes up an attitude based on the prophet *Jonah* from Michelangelo's Sistine Chapel ceiling, a practice which Constable, as a Visitor in the Life Schools in the 1830s, favoured when he posed two male figures based on Michelangelo's *Last Judgement* (Beckett, III, p.37), as well as a setting based on Titian's *St. Peter Martyr* (op. cit., pp.146-7).

It is possible to follow Constable's progress through the successive stages of entry to the Life Class at the Royal Academy with an unusual degree of accuracy. On 25 February 1799 Constable called on Joseph Farington, with a letter of introduction (Farington, IV, p.1164). The following day Farington told him to 'prepare a figure,' that is a drawing from a cast (ibid). Four days later, on 2 March, Constable showed Farington a drawing he had made from the *Belvedere Torso* (op. cit., p.1166). On 4 March Farington gave Constable a letter of

This drawing was traditionally thought to have been executed when Blake was a student at the Royal Academy in 1779-80. Blunt (1959) saw in it the influence of the drawing style of Daniele da Volterra. Keynes (1949) argued that it might be a portrait of Blake's brother Robert. Bindman (1977) suggested that it might be a self-portrait. Its inclusion in the exhibition, among studies of the idealised female body, is designed to focus attention on a drawing in which male attributes are combined with female attitudes derived from the Antique and the Old Masters. The youth's legs are ultimately derived from the *Venus de Medici*, while his arms are derived from poses typical of artists of the Italian Renaissance, (see, for example, the figure to the left in Raphael's *Three Graces* in the right background of *The Wedding Feast of Cupid and Psyche* on the vault of the loggia of the Farnesina). Other female figures' reminiscent of Blake's *Naked Youth* are found in books of engravings in the collection of the Royal Academy, including, for example, Domenico De' Rossi's *Raccolta di Statue Antiche e Moderne* (Rome, 1704) which includes a *Venere uscita dal bagno in atto di asciugarsi*, which is close to the posture of the legs in Blake's drawing. But Blake went further. He produced a new version of the hermaphrodite, an ideal figure for what he called "the Shape of the Naked" in his *Annotations to Sir Joshua Reynold's Discourses* (c.1808; see Keynes, 1969, p.462). A passage in Blake's *Annotations* throws new light on the drawing: 'I was once looking over the Prints from Rafael & Michael Angelo in the Library of the Royal Academy. Moser (the Keeper) came to me & said: "You should not study these old Hard, Stiff & Dry, Unfinish'd Works of Art – Stay a little & I will shew you what you should Study". He went & took down Le Brun's & Ruben's Galleries. How I did secretely Rage! ... I said to Moser, "These things that you call Finish'd are not Even Begun; how can they be Finish'd? The Man who does not know The Beginning never can know the End of Art"' (ibid., p.449). Blake's *Naked Youth* was, it seems, an act of rebellion against the Academy, its educational principles and its orthodox approach to the living model.   I.B.

Venus de Medici   28

J.M.W. TURNER (London 1775-1851)
Chalk and stump on Whatman paper; 37.2 x 26.7 cm
(On verso the front view of a head, unfinished, perhaps of the Venus) c.1790-93

PROVENANCE: Turner Bequest; V/F
LITERATURE: Finberg, 1909, vol.1, p.7
The Tate Gallery, London

Turner was accepted as a student in the Royal Academy Schools in December 1789, on the recommendation of the Academician J.F. Rigaud (1742-1810). Turner attended the Antique Academy regularly until 1793, where his last recorded signature in the 'Plaister Academy' register is on 8 October (Chumbley and Warrell, 1989, p.12). A.J. Finberg counted 137 separate attendances in the Antique Academy by Turner (Finberg, loc. cit.) and it might be implied that this total was even higher, as two registers from the period are missing. Nonetheless only 18 drawings from casts exist among the drawings in the Turner Bequest, which can be dated to Turner's student days (see Finberg, 1909, vol.1, pp.6-8). These include studies of the *Apollo Belvedere*, the *Discobolus*, the Vatican *Meleager*, the *Borghese Gladiator*, the *Belvedere Torso* (see also cat.18) and this work, which is one of two studies of the *Venus de Medici*. Although weak in terms of the realisation of the plastic form of the statue, Turner's study reveals the manner in which the artist has attempted to show the shadows cast by the lamp which illuminated the statue from above. The

Royal Academy possessed a number of different casts of the *Venus de Medici*, and this drawing is from a different one to that shown in Etty's depiction of the female model with the *Venus de Medici* (cat.32), which includes the dolphin and putto on the armature of the marble statue in the Uffizi.   M.P.

Academical study for an *Eve*   29

LOUIS SCHIAVONETTI, after Benjamin West
(Pennsylvania 1738 - London 1820)
Stipple engraving; 62.5 x 44.5 cm

LITERATURE: Kraemer, 1975, pp.61-2, repr.
The Trustees of the British Museum, London

West's drawing, upon which this engraving is based, where the *Venus de Medici* is transformed into a biblical icon by the adjustment of the arms, hair, and the addition of drapery, is signed by the artist, and dated 1784. The following year Horace Walpole noted in a letter to John Pinkerton (16 June 1785): 'Milton had such superior merit, that I will only say, that if his angels, his Satan, and his Adam, have as much dignity as the Apollo Belvedere, his Eve has all the delicacy and graces of the Venus de Medici ...' (Walpole, 1937-83, vol.16, p.270). That West's *Academical Study for an Eve* (the original drawing is lost) was intended as one of a series of didactic life-drawings is suggested by the existence of a highly finished study by West of a male nude seated on a rock, which is signed and dated (1783) in a similar fashion (see Kraemer, 1975, cat.115, pl.72). West's *Academical Study for an Eve* was published in 1814 in *Academical Studies after the Great Masters*, published in 1814 by Minasi.

In 1794, in a Presidential address to the students of the Royal Academy, Benjamin West described how the perfect physical male specimen was embodied in the *Apollo Belvedere*. He continued: 'Were the young artist, in like manner, to propose to himself a subject in which he would endeavour to represent the peculiar excellences of woman, would he not say,

that these excellences consist in a virtuous mind, a modest mien, a tranquil deportment, and a gracefulness in motion? And, in embodying the combined beauties of these qualities, would he not bestow on the figure a general, smooth, and round fulness of form, to indicate the softness of character; bend the head gently forward, in the common attitude of modesty; and awaken our ideas of the slow and graceful movements peculiar to the sex, by limbs free from that masculine and sinewy expression which is the consequence of active exercise? – and such is the Venus de Medici'. (Galt, 1820, p.101).

West's practical application of the figure of the *Venus de Medici* to his own history paintings is seen in *William de Albanac Presenting his Three Daughters (naked) to Alfred, the Third King of Mercia*, of 1778, and *Juno receiving the Cestus from Venus*, exhibited at the Royal Academy in 1772 (von Erffa and Staley, 1986, cats.47 and 169).   M.P.

Female nude, from two angles,   30
in the pose of the *Venus de Medici*
WILLIAM ETTY (York 1787-1849)

Oil on card; 63.4 x 48.3 cm

PROVENANCE: Anonymous gift

EXHIBITED: Rye Art Gallery, 1974 (16); Morley Gallery, London, 1975

LITERATURE: Bailey 1974, repr. pl.8

Courtauld Institute Galleries, London

This oil study by Etty demonstrates the manner in which the living model at the Royal Academy Schools was sometimes required to emulate classical statuary. Here the female model takes up the pose of the *Venus de Medici*, even in the manner in which her hair is caught up behind her neck. The only major

difference is that the pose of the antique statue has been reversed by the Visitor, presumably in the hope that the students would not simply refer back to drawings they had made of the cast, but rather approach the figure with fresh insight.   M.P.

Venus de Medici   31
JOSEPH NOLLEKENS (1737-1823)

Pen and brown ink over pencil, on paper; 44 x 28.2 cm
1770

Inscribed below upper margin: *The hight of this Venus is 7 heads, 3 parts 3 minets; is the work of Cleomene Son of Apollodoro of Athens / each part has 12 minets.*
Also inscribed on verso: *That no doubt of the authenticity or accuracy of these measurements may be / hereafter entertained I now certify that they were taken by me on the real Statue of the Venus De Medici at Florence / in June 1770 Joseph Nollekens.*

PROVENANCE: The Revd Thomas Kerrich; Albert Hartshorne; Oliver E.P. Wyatt; Sotheby's, 7.4.1965, lot 10. Purchased by the Visitors of the Ashmolean Museum, 1965

LITERATURE: Brown, 1982. no.1458

Ashmolean Museum, Oxford

This drawing is one of four known drawings of the *Venus de Medici* by Nollekens, sold by Sotheby's in 1965 (7 April 1965, lot 10), two of which were acquired by the Ashmolean Museum, along with measured drawings of the Capitoline *Antinous* and the *Laocoon*. Nollekens' practice of taking careful measurements from classical statuary stemmed in part from his training in the workshop of the copyist and cast-maker Bartolomeo Cavaceppi in Rome, where precise measurements of original statues were necessary in order to replicate casts for collectors. He would also have experienced this working method at the French Academy in Rome, where the technique of making large-scale copies of antique statuary was also taught (see Haskell and Penny, 1981, 123). Nollekens, we know, made several replicas of classical statues for British collectors,

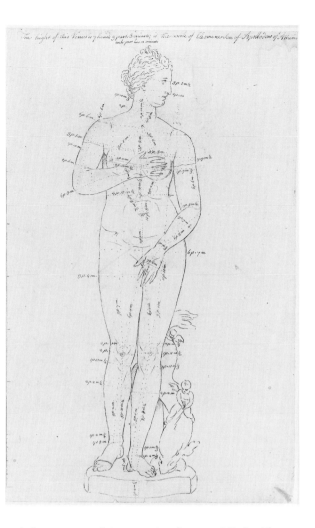

including a copy of *Castor and Pollux* in 1768 for Thomas Anson, which is now in the Victoria and Albert Museum (Kenworthy-Browne, 1979, II, p.1930).

Joseph Nollekens was apprenticed to Peter Scheemackers (1691-1781) in 1750. In 1759 he was awarded a premium from the Society of Arts for a drawing from a plaster cast, and in 1760, for a model in clay. In 1762 he left for Italy. He returned to England eight years later, in October 1770, as a successful and sought-after society sculptor. Most of Nollekens' time was spent in Rome. And, as we can see from his sketchbooks, two of which are in the Ashmolean Museum (Blayney Brown, 1982, nos. 1462 and 1463), he made a habit of studying statuary in the most important galleries including the Vatican, Capitoline, Borghese, and Albani. Nollekens visited the Duke of Tuscany's Gallery in Florence in 1763 when he recorded his admiration for the *Venus de Medici* (Kenworthy-Browne, 1979, I. p.1844). He was there again in June 1770, when he made a series of measured drawings of the same statue.

The system used by Nollekens to measure the *Venus de Medici*, which goes back ultimately to the organic theory of proportions devised by Polycleitos, is closely modelled on that which Gérard Audran had published in 1683 as *Les proportions du corps humain measurées sur les plus belles figures de l'antiquité.* (An English version was first published in 1718). Rather than using a method of measurement based on custom (such as an inch or centimetre) Audran took as his unit of measurement the head of the particular statue. The head was divided into four 'parts,' and each part was subdivided into twelve 'minets'. Audran, who had included two plates of the *Venus de Medici*, from the front and left profile, and the back and right profile, gave the height as seven heads and three parts, whereas Nollekens estimated the total height to be seven heads, three

parts – and three 'minets'. Indeed the very reason Nollekens inscribed each of his drawings with an 'authentification' was presumably to avoid the suspicion that he had merely copied the drawings from Audran. An interesting gloss on Nolleken's measuring activities appears in a picture by Thomas Patch, dated to *c.*1760-70, entitled *A Gathering of Dilettanti round the Venus de Medici* (Sir Brinsley Ford), which includes a figure – thought to be Patch himself – in the act of measuring the *Venus de Medici* with a large pair of dividers (see Ford, 1963, pp.172-6). M.P.

Female nude with a cast of the *Venus de Medici* 32

WILLIAM ETTY (York 1787-1849)

Black and white chalks on brown paper; 56.3 x 38.8 cm
*c.*1833-37

PROVENANCE: Sir Robert Witt

EXHIBITED: Royal Academy 1975 (B51)

LITERATURE: Gilchrist, 1855, vol.2, p.59; Royal Academy 1975, pp.180-81; Chumbley and Warrell, 1989, p.26, no.4; Brown 1990, p.33. repr.

Courtauld Institute Galleries (Witt Collection), London

Etty's drawing of the female model posed with, and imitating the attitude of, the *Venus de Medici* relates to the Visitorship of J.M.W. Turner in the Royal Academy Schools during the mid-1830s. Turner had an abiding interest in the administraton of the Royal Academy, holding Visitorships in the School of Painting, as well as the Professorship of Perspective. In 1820, and again in 1838 and 1839, he was Inspector of the Cast Collection at the Academy, while in October 1833 he was appointed Visitor to the Life Academy, alongside Charles Eastlake, A.E. Chalon, and Abraham Cooper. He was elected to the post again in November 1836. Richard and Samuel Redgrave recalled: 'When a visitor in the life school he introduced a capital practice, which it is to be regretted has not been continued; he chose for study a model as nearly as possible corresponding in form and character with some fine antique figure, which he placed by the side of the model posed in the same action; thus, the *Discobulus of Myron* (sic) contrasted with one of our best trained soldiers; the *Lizard Killer* with a youth in the roundest beauty of adolescence: the *Venus de Medici* beside a female in the first period of youthful womanhood. The idea was original and very instructive: it showed at once how much the antique sculptors had refined nature; which, if in parts more beautiful than the selected form which is called *ideal*, as a whole looked common and vulgar by its side' (Redgrave, 1947, p.256). The idea may have stemmed from Turner's visit in 1819 to an exhibition in the Venetian Academy where Antonio Canova (1757-1822) had arranged living models in attitudes based on antique statuary. Of Turner's actual supervision of the students' work, Ruskin stated; 'In teaching generally, he would neither waste his time, nor spare it; he would look over a student's drawing, at the Academy, – point to a defective part, make a scratch on the paper at the side, saying nothing; if the student saw what was wanted, and did it, Turner was delighted, and would go on with him, giving him hint after hint; but if the student could not follow, Turner left him' (Wilton, 1987, p.178).   M.P.

William Mason copying the *Venus de Medici*   33
FRANCIS MAPLETOFT (1730-1807)

Black paper on white card, with some black pigment; 47.5 x 35 cm
c.1765

PROVENANCE: Possibly presented by the sitter to Pembroke College

EXHIBITED: York 1973 (47)

LITERATURE: Gray 1935, II, p.xxxiii, repr. facing p.796; Barr and Ingamells, 1973, no.21

Pembroke College, Cambridge

In the silhouette exhibited here, William Mason (1725-1797), is shown drawing from a reduced copy of the *Venus de Medici*. He never saw the original statue, not having made the Grand Tour. Reduced copies of classical statuary were very common by the 18th century. The artist David Allan, is shown painting from a small cast of the *Borghese Gladiator* in the portrait by Domenico Corvi, in the exhibition (see cat.10), while Mrs Daniel Wray, in a silhouette of the Wray Family of 1766 (Private Collection) included a reduced cast of the same sculpture (Hickman, 1973, p.1790, repr.).
    William Mason was born in 1725, the son of a clergyman. In 1742 he went up to Cambridge, where he acquired an interest in poetry, and formed friendships with Richard Hurd, William Warburton and William Whitehead. Denied his father's inheritance, Mason entered the Church in 1754, obtaining a preferment in York and, in 1757, the post of Royal Chaplain. Although he is known today chiefly for his poem, *The English Garden* (1772-9), Mason was a genuine polymath with an interest in science, social issues, and the Fine Arts. He was a good friend of Sir Joshua Reynolds, and left a valuable record of Reynolds' studio practice, as well as a translation of Du

Fresnoy's *Art of Painting* (1783), to which Reynolds appended notes. The Rev. Francis Mapletoft, like Mason before him, was elected a Fellow of Pembroke College in 1754. The silhouette was probably produced by drawing an outline around a shadow cast by the figure onto a sheet of paper. The image would then have been reduced mechanically using a pantograph, or similar device (Barr and Ingamells, 1973, p.25).   M.P.

Study for *Design*   34
ANGELICA KAUFFMAN (Coire 1740 - Rome 1807)

Oil on paper; 22.3 x 27.5 cm
c.1779-80

PROVENANCE: Earl of Warwick sale, Christies, 20-21 May, 1896 (Lugt 2600)

LITERATURE: Manners and Williamson, 1924, p.130

The Board of Trustees, Victoria and Albert Museum, London

The *Belvedere Torso* held a special place among the specimens of classical statuary revered by European artists, not least because it was thought that Michelangelo had found in it 'a certain principle' which 'gave his works a grandeur of gusto equal to the best antiques' (quoted in Haskell and Penny, 1981, pp.312-3). As a result the *Torso* came to symbolise the art of Sculpture and featured prominently in a host of allegories of the visual arts including this example until the mid-19th century (op. cit., p.313). Kauffman's finished painting, which is based on the present sketch, wa one of four roundels – 'Design', 'Composition', 'Genius', and 'Painting' – produced by the artist to decorate the ceiling of New Somerset House in 1780 (and which were subsequently transferred to the Academy's current headquarters at Burlington House).

This study has a particular poignancy because Angelica Kauffman, as a woman, could not work from the living model at the Royal Academy, even though she was a founder member (see cat.5). J.T. Smith, who had heard that Kauffman had arranged private sessions with a Royal Academy model named Charles Cranmer, went round to see him to find out if this was true. Cranmer told Smith that 'he did frequently sit before Angelica Kauffman at her home on the south side of Golden Square, but that he had only exposed his arms, shoulders, and legs, and that her father, who was also an artist and likewise an exhibitor at the Academy, was always present' (Smith, 1828, vol.1, p.65). This sketch makes an interesting comparison with Nathaniel Dance's watercolour of Kauffman (National Gallery of Scotland) where she is shown drawing from a small-scale male cast, i.e. here.   M.P.

Emma Hamilton in classical attitude (*see cat.35*)

Emma Hamilton in classical attitude   35

RICHARD COSWAY (Tiverton 1742 - London 1821)
Pencil and watercolour; 22.2 x 14 cm
*c.*1800

PROVENANCE: Bequeathed by H.W. Murray in 1938

EXHIBITED: Bregenz and Vienna, 1968-9; Kenwood, 1972 (92); Scottish National Portrait Gallery, 1978 (53)

LITERATURE: Jaffe, 1972, no.92; Bennett and Stevenson, 1978, pp.53-57; Yung, 1981, no.2941; Fraser, 1986, repr.

National Portrait Gallery, London

At the time of Cosway's drawing, Emma Hart (1765?-1815) was already famous for the 'Attitudes' she performed after classical statuary during her sojourn in Italy as the mistress of Sir William Hamilton, the British Ambassador in Naples. The first record of Emma's 'Attitudes' was in 1787 when Goethe, who was at the time a guest at Sir William Hamilton's residence noted: 'He has had a Greek costume made for her which becomes her extremely. Dressed in this, she lets down her hair and, with a few shawls, gives so much variety to her poses, gestures, expressions, etc., that the spectator can hardly believe his eyes ... The old knight (Hamilton) idolises her and is quite enthusiastic about everything she does. In her he has found all the antiquities, all the profiles of Sicilian coins, even the *Apollo Belvedere*' (Fraser, 1986, p.121). In 1794 Frederick Rehberg produced a series of line engravings of Emma's 'Attitudes' entitled *Drawings Faithfully Copied from Nature at Naples*. In 1800 she returned to England, around which time Cosway produced this drawing. By this time she was, according to one contemporary, 'colossal, but, excepting her feet, which are hideous, well shaped. Her bones are large, and she is exceedingly *embonpoint*. She resembles the bust of Ariadne ...' (Fraser, 1986, p.270). Emma continued to perform her 'Attitudes' in the early 1800s, although in 1807, owing to her 'enormous size' a set of engravings were published which cruelly caricatured Rehberg's early series. They were published as *A New edition, considerably enlarged, of Attitudes faithfully copied from Nature ...; Studies of Academic Attitudes*. She died in Calais, impoverished and alcoholic, in January 1815.   M.P.

The Sculptor   36

THOMAS ROWLANDSON (London 1756-1827)
Engraving, coloured impression; 28 x 22.3 cm
*c.*1800

LITERATURE: Grego, 1880, vol.2, pp.16-19; George, 1942, no.9572

The Trustees of the British Museum, London

Although Rowlandson's print was not produced until *c.*1800, the clay *modello* on which Nollekens is shown at work, *Venus chiding Cupid,* was apparently exhibited at the Royal Academy in 1778 (Gunnis, 1968, p.277). Even though Rowlandson's print is essentially a satirical flight of fancy, the image anticipates the recollections of Nollekens's pupil, J.T. Smith, concerning the sculptor's primary interest in the studio, rather than the academy, model. According to Smith, 'his naked figures were of the most simple class, being either a young Bacchus, a Diana, or a Venus, with limbs sleek, plump, and round; but I never knew him like Banks, to attempt the grandeur of a Jupiter, or even the strength of a gladiator ... Nollekens's large academical drawings, made when he was Visitor in the Royal Academy, were feebly executed, his men were destitute of animation, and his females lame in their joints; their faces were usually finished up at home from his

wife, and in compliment to her, he generally contrived to give them little noses' (Smith, 1828, vol.2, p.12).

Aside from his satirical depictions of academies (see cat.67) Rowlandson produced a number of other artist-and-model prints including *Intrusion on Study, or the Painter disturbed* (George, no.6862) which depicts a group of men bursting in on a male artist and his naked female model, and *Lady Hxxxxxxx Attitudes* (George, no.9571) which alluded to Emma Hamilton's supposed private activities as an artist's model. Even in old age Nollekens was not immune to the charms of his own female models, as Smith recalled: 'He continued now and then to amuse himself with his modelling-clay, and frequently gave tea and other entertainments to some of his old models, who generally left his house a bank-note or two richer than they arrived. Indeed, so stupidly childish was he at times, that one of his Venuses, who had grown old in her practices, coaxed him out of ten pounds to enable her to make him a plum pudding' (Smith, 1828, vol.1, p.318).   M.P.

The Analysis of Beauty (Plate I)   37
WILLIAM HOGARTH (London 1697-1764)

Engraving; 38.7 x 48.3 cm
1753

PROVENANCE: Prof V. de Sola Pinto

LITERATURE: Burke, 1955; Dobai, 1968; Paulson, 1971, vol.2, pp.168-71; Friedman & Clifford, 1974, no.1; Bignamini, 1988, pl.79; Bindman 1981; Paulson, 1989

University Art Gallery, Nottingham

The scene depicted by Hogarth in the first plate of his *Analysis of Beauty*, is probably the celebrated statuary yard of John Cheere (1709-87) on Hyde Park Corner, where, as the artist noted at the time, casts taken from famous antique statuary were more fêted than their modern counterparts (see Haskell and Penny, 1981, p.80). Among the casts which feature prominently in Hogarth's engraving are, from left to right,

bust-length and full-length versions of the *Farnese Hercules*, the *Belvedere Antinous*, the *Laocoon* (in the background by the gate), the *Venus de Medici*, the *Belvedere Torso* (the plinth of which bears the signature of the sculptor Apollonius) and the *Apollo Belvedere*. All the statues are shown in reverse, although they would obviously have been the right way round in Hogarth's original drawing.

In addition to the contemporary reference to Cheere's statuary yard Hogarth indirectly alluded to the statuary yard of the classical sculptor Clito, where Socrates apparently went to illustrate his theories on beauty with reference to the statues around him (see Paulson, 1971, vol.2, p.168). Like Socrates, Hogarth also used the scenario as a backdrop for his own ideas on the human figure. In the left foreground, for example, is an anatomical engraving showing three flayed legs (see also cat.84). Hogarth referred to the legs in Chapter IX of the *Analysis of Beauty* in order to illustrate his ideas on 'composition with the waving line'. Here the 'elegant forms composed of serpentine lines' in the middle leg (65) are compared to the 'sticky manner' of the leg to the right (66) and the 'wooden form' of the leg to the left (67) (Burke, 1955, pp.72-73). The middle leg, preferred by Hogarth, was apparently drawn from a plaster cast made by William Cowper (1660-1709), the famous British surgeon, and author of *The Anatomy of Human Bodies* (1697). Cowper was also a draughtsman in his own right and a one-time member of the club of Virtuosi of St. Luke (Bignamini 1988B, 1).

The illustrations in the drawing books in the right foreground were, as Burke observed (ibid., p.91), based on theories of proportion found in the works of Albrecht Dürer and Giampolo Lomazzo. (For Dürer and Lomazzo see Bolten, 1985, pp.169-75 and pp.176-78). Hogarth had little use for the dry, formulaic approach to the figure put forward in theoretical treatises. When, for example, he discussed the female figure as represented in didactic texts he commented: 'who but a bigot even to the antiques, will say that he has not seen faces and necks, hands and arms in living women, that even the *Grecian Venus* doth but coarsely imitate?' (Burke, p.82). Hogarth's ideas were, however, increasingly out of tune with those of his peers, who wished to assimilate their own views with those promulgated by European artists and theorists.   M.P

An Academy 38

WILLIAM PETHER after Joseph Wright
(Derby 1734-97)

Mezzotint engraving; 58 x 45.5 cm
Inscribed: Ios*h*, Wright, Pinx*t* W Pether, Fecit

LITERATURE: Nicolson, 1968, vol.1, p.234; Egerton, 1990, p.240

Hon. Christopher Lennox-Boyd

Joseph Wright exhibited *An Academy by Lamplight* at the Society of Artists in 1769 (197) (Egerton, 1990, cat.23). The engraving, a second state of which is exhibited here, was made by William Pether and published on 25 February 1772 (op. cit., cat. p.9). As in Elias Martin's *Cast Room at the Royal Academy* (cat.6), the presence of youths rather than men is stressed, perhaps in order to make the point that the study of the antique was the basis of all subsequent artistic education. It is almost certain that Wright's *Academy* is imaginary, not least because the work is didactic rather than descriptive in its intention to show that the ideal of physical perfection is personified not by the living individual, but by the paradigm offered by the antique. Wright, who did not visit Italy until 1773, must have taken his images of the *Nymph with a Shell* (then in the Villa Borghese) and the *Borghese Gladiator* (see Haskell and Penny, 1981, cats.67 and 43) from casts rather than the original antique statues. He would, of course, have been able to draw and observe casts under similar conditions at the Duke of Richmond's Sculpture Gallery. He also obviously had access to a reduced version of the *Borghese Gladiator* which featured in *Three Persons Viewing the Gladiator by Candle-light*, which Wright exhibited at the Society of Artists in 1765 (see Egerton, 1990, cat.22). M.P.

The Antique Room, New Somerset House 39

EDWARD FRANCESCO BURNEY
(Worcester 1760 - London 1848)

Pen and coloured wash on paper; 33.6 x 48.9 cm
1780

PROVENANCE: from an album containing drawings by various members of the Burney family; Colnaghi, from whom it was bought by the Royal Academy (Sydney Lee Fund) in 1960

LITERATURE: Crown, 1977, p.15

Royal Academy of Arts, London

A companion drawing to *The Antique Room, Old Somerset House* of 1779 (fig.3), this work is contemporary with *The Antique School of the Royal Academy at New Somerset House* (cat.6). It shows the other side of the room. Yet compared to the painting, the drawing is less didactic. The Antique Academy is shown here as a quiet room, where both senior and junior students work unsupervised. Casts shown include, from the left to right: *Cincinnatus*, the *Dying Gladiator*, the *Venus de Medici*, *Cupid and Psyche*, the *Capitoline Antinous* and the *Uffizi Mercury* (Haskell and Penny, 1981, nos. 5, 23, 26, 44, 61, 88). To the right of the *Dying Gladiator* is a cast of the *Nymph 'alla Spina'* (Bober and Rubinstein, 1986, no.61). I.B.

Fig.3 EDWARD BURNEY *The Antique School at Old Somerset House*, 1779
Pen and coloured wash, Royal Academy of Arts

Cast Room of the Royal Academy   40

Attributed to FRANCIS WHEATLEY   (COL PLATE XII)
(London 1747-1801)

Oil on canvas; 43.1 x 53.3 cm
c.1795-1800

PROVENANCE: ? Joseph Mayer; Bebingon Borough Council
(Mayer Trust); presented to Lady Lever Art Gallery 1949

Trustees of the National Museums and Galleries on
Merseyside, Lady Lever Art Gallery, Port Sunlight

This unfinished painting shows the Cast Room of the Royal
Academy. Three statues are identifiable. They are, from left to
right, the Capitoline *Antinous*, the *Apollo Belvedere,* and the
Laocoon. Although the date is not known the style of dress
would suggest the second half of the 1790s. The attribution of
this picture to Francis Wheatley must remain tentative.
Wheatley had been elected a Royal Academician in February
1791, and in 1794 he was appointed a Visitor in the Academy
Schools. By then, however, he had fallen on hard times. In
January 1795 he was forced to sell his house, and his personal
property, including sixty plaster casts after the Antique
(Webster, 1970, p.105). And by 1796 he was, in addition, in
very poor health, much of his time being spent convalescing in
Bath. His last oils were painted in 1799, by which time he was
severely crippled. He died on 28 June 1801.   M.P.

The Temporary Elgin Room   41
at the British Museum

ARCHIBALD ARCHER (1789/90 - London 1848)

Oil on canvas; 76.2 x 102.7 cm
Signed and dated: *A. Archer, 1819*

PROVENANCE: Edward Hawkins; Dr J.E. Gray, who presented
it to the British Museum in 1872

EXHIBITED: Arts Council, 1972 (10)

LITERATURE: Smith, 1916, pp.353-55, fig.16; Thompson
1961; Ashmole, 1964, p.37, pl.37; St. Clair, 1967, fig.IX;
Cook, 1984, pp.66-7, repr.

The Trustees of the British Museum, London

This painting was exhibited at the British Institution in 1819
(Graves, 1875, no.53). It shows the room in which the Elgin
Marbles, including the most important pedimental sculptures
and metopes from the Parthenon (Cook, 1984, passim), were
exhibited to the public between 1817 and 1831. The bas-reliefs
and statuary were removed from the Acropolis and shipped
to England between 1801 and 1811, and formed part of the
collection of antiquities assembled by Thomas Bruce, 7th
Earl of Elgin (1766-1841), during his diplomatic mission
to Constantinople between 1801-3. They had been
accommodated first at the house of the Duchesss of Portland in
Westminster, and subsequently in a shed in Park Lane (see
cat.25), where in June 1808, a well-known boxer, named
Gregson, was 'placed in many attitudes', in order to compare
them with figures in the Marbles (Farington, IX, p.3306). In
1811 Elgin offered the Marbles to the nation for £62,440. After
a prolonged Parliamentary inquiry, they were purchased from
him in 1816 for £35,000, and handed over to the British
Museum. The painter of this work, Archibald Archer, is shown
seated in right foreground. The President of the Royal
Academy, Benjamin West, is seated at the left, while to his right
is Joseph Planta, Principal Librarian at the British Museum.
Benjamin Robert Haydon, the most fervent advocate of the
Marbles, is standing, in profile, at the extreme left.   I.B./M.P.

(Shown at Kenwood only)

III   The Living Model

The material in this section illustrates the different ways in which artists perceived the living model between the 1710s and the 1830s. A selection of nude male and female Academy figures has been made to emphasis stylistic similarities between artists working during the same period, and to demonstrate also the changes which took place from the early-18th to the first quarter of the 19th century. As well as studies of individual models, there are also pictures of artists at work in the Life Class and the studio – both serious and satirical. The employment of models in academies of art is documented in England as early as 1673, although it was only after the Academy in Great Queen Street was established in 1711 that academic life drawings played an important role in the development of a common 'grammar' for the British School. The practice of communal drawing of the model, at first the male only, and after 1720 the male and female model, enabled the cosmopolitan community of artists active in London during the first half of the 18th century to conceive of a national school of painters, draughtsmen and engravers.

Colour Plate XIII   WILLIAM ETTY *Two male nudes, seated, c.1815-18*
Nottingham Castle Museum and Art Gallery (cat.54)

Male nude seated in profile to right, 42
with legs crossed, pointing to his board

ELISHA KIRKALL (Sheffield 1682 - London 1742)
after Louis Chéron (Paris 1660 - London 1725)

Etching, woodcut and mezzotint; 23.6 x 30.1 cm
Inscribed: *L: Chéron delin.* (left) and *E: Kirkall fec.* (right). BM
Foreign Masters in England C11*
1735

The Trustees of the British Museum, London

A comparison between Kirkall's print and the original drawing
by Chéron (fig.4) shows how, by the addition of a little
vegetation and a few rocks, an academy nude might turn into
an historical composition. This was an approach to the nude
that Louis Chéron had learned at the *Académie Royale de
Peinture et de Sculpture* in Paris and at the French Academy in
Rome. Settings in Chéron's Roman nudes (red chalk drawings
in the British Museum album, see Croft-Murray and Hulton,
1960, p.280, nos. 92-99, ill.8) are similar to the setting in
Kirkall's print. According to George Vertue (III, p.22) Chéron
was much imitated by young students who attended the
Academy in Great Queen Street, 1711-20. One such student
was Kirkall, who in 1735 advertised six academy figures in
'chiaro obscuro' after the drawings of the late Louis Chéron in
Fog's Weekly Journal (15 March 1735; price 4s). The print
selected for this exhibition is one of these. Vertue does not

Fig.4 LOUIS CHERON *Male nude, in profile*
blackchalk, heightened with white, on paper c.1711-24
The Trustees of the British Museum

refer to engravings by Kirkall after Chéron's academy figures.
However, he mentions '6 prints after Mons.r Chéron's
Academy figures' engraved by Gerard Vandergucht (Vertue VI,
p.189; also VI, p.188 and III, p.7). Vandergucht also attended
the Academy of 1711. A third artist, George Bickham Jr.
(Hammelmann, 1975), is known to have produced at least one
engraving after an academy figure by Chéron. It shows a
reclining male nude seen from the rear and is inscribed 'L.
Chéron delin. G. Bickham jun.r ex. in May's Buildings Co.t
Garden'. The plate measures 23.6 x 30.8 cm., almost the same
size as Kirkall's. No date is given for Vandergucht's set or
Bockham's print. Kirkall's advertisement of 1735 can only
suggest a possible date: it may not have been the first to
appear.

The dissemination of Chéron's academy figures suggests
that the French artist played a crucial role in English art
education from 1711 to 1735 at least. His rigorous life-studies
offered an alternative to illustrations of the male figure in
drawing books. Reaction to second-hand copies available in
copy-books was in the air in the early 1730s. In 1729-31 Sir
James Thornhill executed a series of 162 drawings of details of
the Raphael *Cartoons* at Hampton Court with the intention of
publishing them for the use of art students (Lambert, 1981,
p.27, no.60). Kirkall's *Male Nude* is one of many instances
which suggests that new 'printed models' for the artist were
produced in early 18th-century England as a consequence of
the establishment of private academies. Kirkall went to
London when he was about 20 years old; he studied at the
Academy of 1711 and was a member of the Rose and Crown
Club (Bignamini, 1988B, 2, 3); later, he worked for Jacob
Tonson (Hammelmann, 1975).

I am grateful to David Alexander for help in preparing
this entry. I.B.

Male nude seated in profile to right, 43
drawing on a board

LOUIS CHÉRON (Paris 1660 - London 1725)

Black chalk heightened with white on grey paper; 64.8 x 56.2 cm
1711-12

PROVENANCE: From an album of drawings by Chéron
assembled by James, 10th Earl of Derby; by family descent to
Edward, 18th Earl of Derby; bought by the British Museum
at the sale of his collection, Christie's, London, 19.10.1953,
lot 1.

EXHIBITED: British Museum, 1987 (173)

LITERATURE: Croft-Murray and Hulton 1960, p.279, no.86;
Stainton and White 1987, no.173

The Trustees of the British Museum, London

This drawing is the companion of the *Nude male seated*
engraved by Kirkall after Chéron in 1735 (cat. 42 and fig.4).
The model is possibly the pugilist James Figg (cat. 69). The
pose is reminiscent of Michelangelo's *Prophets* and *Sibyls* in the
Sistine Chapel. The rendering of scientific anatomy is more
strongly felt than in nudes drawn by artists at the French
Academy in Rome (ill.8). There they are invested with
anatomical features derived from the Old Masters, especially
Annibale Carracci (ill.7). Chéron arrived in London in 1695.
From 1711 to 1724 he was involved in academies established in
London. Chéron imported into England teaching methods in
use at academies in France and Italy, concentrating his
attention on high quality academy nudes and the rendering of
anatomical features. They were, moreover, very different from
academy nudes executed by portraitists such as Sir Godfrey
Kneller, the first Governor of the Academy in Great Queen

This drawing, which was probably executed in Italy, is one of only a very few existing drawings after the living model by Giles Hussey, who was renowned by the late 1730s for his talent as a draughtsman. The attitude of the model, which is highly unusual – and uncomfortable – was probably devised in order to acquaint the artist with the foreshortenings and distortions of the human form necessary in the production of history painting. In 1732, only two years after Hussey had departed for Italy, George Vertue reported: 'From Bologna news, that Giles Hussey of (sic) had gaind a prize in the accademy their of Painting last year & this year gaind another, that he is gone to Rome Naples Venice &c, to finish his studies' (Vertue III, p.64). While in Italy Hussey drew from the cast (see cat.22) and from the living model, as well as studying anatomy (Vertue, III, p.103). In 1737 Vertue noted that Hussey had returned from Italy, commenting that he had 'spent most of his time only in drawing – little or no painting' (op. cit., p.80). Although Hussey showed great promise he failed to live up to expectations. He produced relatively few finished pictures, and preferred to devote his time to theory rather than practice (see Vertue, III, p.127 for a discussion of Hussey's artistic theories).   M.P.

Street, whose drawings (ill.4) show a primary interest in poses rather than the actual bodies of the models. In their turn, Chéron's academy nudes were modified by the English Life Class and by William Cheselden who attended the Academy of 1720 (see cat.74).   I.B.

Male nude, reclining on board   **44**
GILES HUSSEY (1710-88)

Graphite on off-white paper; 23.3x18.5cm
c.1730-7

PROVENANCE: Earl of Gainsborough; Sir Robert Witt

Courtauld Institute Galleries (Witt collection), London

Male nude seated, with left arm raised   **45**
JOSEPH HIGHMORE
(London 1692 - Canterbury 1780)

Pencil, pen and grey wash on paper; 24x19cm, pasted on paper; 27x20cm

PROVENANCE: Part of a collection of sketches, drawings, watercolours and other material by Joseph Highmore, his daughter Susan, later Mrs. Duncombe, and other relatives presented to the Tate Gallery by Mrs. Jean Highmore Blacknall and Dr. R.B. McConnell in 1986

LITERATURE: Einberg and Egerton, 1988, p.71, no.84

The Trustees of the Tate Gallery, London

The dating of academy drawings is notoriously difficult. A number of elements must be taken into account including the medium and paper used, size, the artist's drawing style as it develops during his career, his studio training, his membership of academies, the physiognomy of the model (and his or her distinctive anatomical features), and finally the model's pose and paraphernalia depicted in the drawing. Highmore's *Male nude seated* is a good example of a drawing which raises such problems. Nonetheless it can be stated confidently that this drawing and its companion (Einberg and Egerton, 1988, p.71, no.83) were not executed from the life at an academy of art. Rather, with its high degree of finish, it looks to have been made as an illustration for an unexecuted theoretical treatise. Highmore attended the Academy in Great Queen Street and the first St. Martin's Lane Academy (Bignamini 1988B, 3 and 4). But, like many artists of his generation, he also drew from the living model at the second St. Martin's Lane Academy. Information given by Vertue in his notebooks about artist-members of this Academy is fragmentary and no records of the Academy have come to light so far. A conjectural dating for Highmore's drawing can, however, be suggested. The artist's drawing style, the medium he used, his handling of anatomy and the model's pose suggest a date not earlier than 1744, when Highmore painted *The Good Samaritan* (Tate Gallery; Einberg and Egerton, 1988, pp.60-61, no.24).   I.B.

G.M. Moser.

Male nude   46
GEORGE MICHAEL MOSER
(Schaffhausen c.1704 - London 1783)
Red chalk on paper; 57 x 38 cm
? c.1745-50

PROVENANCE: Possibly presented by the artist to the Royal Academy

Royal Academy of Arts, London

Although George Michael Moser was active in the Life Class throughout his career, few of his own life drawings survive. As Moser is not known to have worked either in Paris or Rome, it is probable that this drawing was made in London in the St. Martin's Lane Academy, possibly in the 1740s. Indeed, the use of red chalk for life-drawings in England was probably far more common than has hitherto been recognised. Several drawings by Allan Ramsay, for example, which may have been made in St. Martin's Lane in the later 1750s, employ a similar medium and technique (see cat.58). Moser was known for his abilities as a draughtsman and George Vertue, writing in 1745 about the St. Martin's Lane Academy, noted that 'amongst the best Mr. Moser the Chaser has distinguisht him self by his skill in drawing in ye Academy from the life this Winter' (Vertue, III, p.123).

Moser's early history is obscure. He is said to have studied in Geneva before coming to England as a youth to work as a gold- and silver-chaser. Moser also worked as an enameller, medallist, and sculptor. He is known to have been involved in the St. Martin's Lane Academy as Treasurer and as a Director in 1747. He was also involved in 1755 in negotiations for the establishment of an Academy with the Society of Dilettanti. By 1766 he was a Director of the Incorporated Society of Artists. Moser was also instrumental in the foundation of the Royal Academy of Arts, and became its first Keeper in 1769. In that post, it was his responsibility to oversee the running of the 'Academy of the Living Model' and the 'Plaister Academy', including the provision of models, the setting out of the casts, and the admission of new students to the Schools. (For Moser's encounter with Rowlandson in the Life Class see cat.67).   M.P.

Male nude, reclining   47
JOHN HAMILTON MORTIMER
(Eastbourne 1740 – London 1779)
Black chalk, heightened with white, on paper; 20.6 x 37 cm
c.1757-9

PROVENANCE: Purchased 1887

LITERATURE: Sunderland, 1986, p.122, no.5

The Board of Trustees, Victoria and Albert Museum, London

John Hamilton Mortimer was the most precocious draughtsman of his generation. While a pupil of Robert Edge Pine (1730-88) he studied at the St. Martin's Lane Academy, and at the Duke of Richmond's Sculpture Gallery, winning prizes both for life drawing and for a drawing from a cast of Michelangelo's *Bacchus* (Society of Arts). As Sunderland observes (Sunderland 1986, p.6), Mortimer enjoyed the informal atmosphere of the drawing schools and academies far more than life in the studio of either Pine or his first master, Thomas Hudson. The medium used by Mortimer in this drawing, black chalk on grey paper, and the technique, with firm cross-hatching, is very close to that which the artist employed in drawings from the Antique. Nonetheless, although the drawing exhibits Mortimer's control of line and his confident manipulation of tone, it also reveals the difficulties he experienced in coping with the unexpected irregularities of the human form as opposed to the familiar contours of the classical cast – especially in the handling of the area around the upper torso and neck. This work has much in common, stylistically, with two life drawings by Mortimer in an album of life drawings by British artists (including William Pars, Lewis Pingo, and John Keyes Sherwin) in the Society of Arts. Mortimer's drawings in the Society of Arts (Sunderland, nos. 2 and 3) are dated by the artist 1758 and 1759 respectively, and were probably made at the St. Martin's Lane Academy. This drawing would seem to date from the same period and venue. Although the technique is different from Cipriani's sheet of studies (cat.49), and Wilson's drawing of a reclining male nude (cat.48), the similarity of pose suggests perhaps that it was done within Cipriani's orbit.   M.P.

Recumbent male nude   48

RICHARD WILSON (Penegoes ? 1713 - Llanberis 1782)

Black chalk, heightened with white, on grey paper; 40 x 57.8 cm

PROVENANCE: Purchased by the National Museum of Wales from Colnaghi, May 1945

LITERATURE: Borenius, 1944, pp.211-13; Constable, 1953, p.163, pl.21a; Gage, 1987, p.107 repr.

National Museum of Wales, Cardiff

This drawing is a study for one of the central figures in *The Destruction of Niobe's Children* (Yale Center for British Art) which Wilson exhibited at the Society of Artists in 1760. Wilson had been among the founders of the Incorporated Society of Artists in 1759, as well as a member of the St. Martin's Lane Academy, where the present study was probably made. (For a comparison with similar studies by Cipriani see cat.49). Wilson's *Niobe* was the central work in his *oeuvre* (Solkin, 1982, p.200). Although Wilson based the nude here on a study taken from life, the figure of Niobe was based on the *Niobe Group* (Haskell and Penny, 1981, cat.66), which Wilson had sketched in 1752 (Solkin, 1982, p.201). Solkin notes that the adaptation of classical statuary to Wilson's figure of Niobe was particularly appropriate as, according to Ovid, Niobe was herself turned into stone by Apollo and Diana (loc. cit.).

Wilson had spent the years from 1750 to around 1756 in Italy. Although he increasingly turned his attention to landscape during this period, he is known to have been a member of the *Accademia del Nudo* in Rome (see McDonald, in Boschloo et al., 1989, pp.80-81), where he produced a number of life drawings (see Ford, 1951, pp.25 and 39).   M.P.

Four studies of a recumbent male nude   49

GIOVANNI BATTISTA CIPRIANI
(Florence 1727 - London 1785)

Pen, ink and was on paper; 47.6 x 34.3 cm
c.1758-60

PROVENANCE: With Kaye Dowland Mansfield from 1862 to 1921, when purchased by A.P. Oppé; by descent to present owner

Private Collection

This series of studies of a recumbent male figure is close enough, in terms of the attitude of the model, to Richard Wilson's study for *Niobe* (see cat.48) to suggest that they were executed around the same time at the Academy in St. Martin's Lane. Cipriani must have known Wilson well. Born in Florence, Cipriani had spent the years 1750 to 1753 in Rome, where he had come into close contact with the British artistic community including the architect William Chambers (1729-96), the sculptor Joseph Wilton (1722-1803) – and, we can assume, Richard Wilson. In 1756 Cipriani went to London, where, in addition to carrying out a number of decorative paintings for Chambers and Robert Adam, he joined Wilton as an instructor at the Duke of Richmond's Cast Gallery. Cipriani had an abiding interest in art education. He became a member of the St. Martin's Lane Academy, and was subsequently a founder member of the Royal Academy, where he was prominent as a teacher.   M.P.

Male nude (study for *The Good Samaritan*)   50

FRANCIS HAYMAN (Exeter 1708 - London 1776)
c.1751

Black chalk, heightened with white, on buff paper; 47.6 x 59.4 cm

PROVENANCE: Possibly presented to the Royal Academy by the artist

EXHIBITIONS: Yale and Kenwood, 1987 (70)

LITERATURE: Allen, 1987, p.139

Royal Academy of Arts, London

This drawing is a study for the naked figure in Hayman's oil painting, *The Good Samaritan* (Yale Center for British Art), which the artist painted for the Chapel at Cusworth Hall (see Allen, 1987, no.47). Hayman's drawing, which is the only extant study from the naked living model by the artist, is also one of the few mid 18th-century British drawings which relates to a known historical composition. Probably executed at the second St. Martin's Lane Academy, Hayman's drawing raises some very interesting questions about the use of the living model in the Academy other than as an academic exercise. There is, in fact, one recorded precedent for the use of the model in the Academy for a particular historical composition. In or around 1713, at an evening session at Kneller's Academy, Sir James Thornhill placed the model in a 'curious crouching position' for a figure he wished to incorporate into the ceiling of the Painted Hall at Greenwich. The principal difference, however, between Hayman's practice and Thornhill's, was that the latter was not actually in attendance at the Academy on the evening in question, having instructed another artist, Thomas Gibson (c.1680-1751) to pose the model and execute the drawings for him (see Whitley, 1928, vol.1, p.13).   I.B./M.P.

Male nude, resting on a waterspout   51
ALLAN RAMSAY (Edinburgh 1713 - Dover 1784)

Black chalk, heightened with white, on paper; 28.2 x 42 cm
Inscribed on the verso in Ramsay's hand: *French Accadm, by day light, Dec 11 1755.*

PROVENANCE: General John Ramsay; Lady Murray gift 1860

LITERATURE: Andrews and Brotchie, 1960, D. 3798; Fleming 1956, p.84, pl.11

The National Galleries of Scotland, Edinburgh

One of a series of drawings made in natural light by Ramsay at the French Academy in Rome, during his second visit to Italy (1754-1755). Ramsay had first visited the French Academy during his earlier Italian sojourn (1736-1738), where he is recorded as having studied the living model in the evening by lamplight (Smart, 1956, p.29). He continued to draw from the living model on his return to England, at St. Martin's Lane, where he was criticised by George Vertue (see Vertue III, p.96). Critically, Ramsay fared little better on his return to Rome in the 1750s, when Andrew Lumisden told the engraver Robert Strange that Ramsay 'drew such figures as everyone laughed at and wondered how he could pretend to be a painter' (quoted by MacDonald, 1989, p.78). Another fellow-Scot, Robert Adam also observed, in 1756: 'There are many qualities and studys (sic) that form a good painter that he is ignorant of as an unborn child, and he for an old boy knows less about the proportions of the human figure than any young boy about Rome, a fact which amazed and astonished me' (Fleming, 1956, p.81).

Despite criticism Ramsay continued to draw from the model at the St. Martin's Lane Academy (there is, for example, a drawing in the National Gallery of Scotland of a reclining female nude inscribed: 'St. Martin's Lane, Novr 1758', Andrews and Brotchie 1960, D.2209). One problem however, for a busy portraitist like Ramsay must have been that the practice of life drawing was not integrated into his everyday artistic practice. Nonetheless, as has been pointed out (MacDonald, in Boschloo et al., 1989, p.78) the drawings which survive from both Ramsay's first and second trips to Italy indicate that the artist rapidly gained in confidence as he drew from the model.   M.P.

(University Art Gallery, Nottingham only)

Male nude, standing, from rear   52
JOHN JAMES MASQUERIER
(London 1778 - Brighton 1855)

Black chalk and stump, heightened with white, on buff paper; 57.8 x 41.9 cm
Inscribed: *the last drawing from nature at Paris*
1792

PROVENANCE: D.E., Forbes (Masquerier's descendant); sold Christie's 19.1.1878, bought Baroness Burdett-Couts, lot 75; W.A.B. Burdett-Coutts; his sale, Christie's 4.5.1922; bought by the Wellcome Institute

LITERATURE: Sée, 1922, pp.14-15

Wellcome Institute Library, London

This is one of a fascinating series of 56 drawings by Masquerier in the Wellcome Institute Library, which chart the artist's progress in art schools in Paris and London, working both from the life, and after the Antique, during the period 1790 to 1793. Of Huguenot descent, Masquerier was born in London, where soon after his birth, his father sold the family's silversmithing business. In 1788 faced with the prospect of bankruptcy, Masquerier's mother decided to open a school in Paris. In 1789 Masquerier was sent to study in the *Académie Royale*, which was then under the Directorship of François-Andre Vincent (1746-1816). While in Paris he also studied in the atélier of Carle Vernet (1758-1836). It has been suggested that Masquerier enrolled at the Royal Academy Schools in 1789. The artist himself later claimed that he had, as a youth, been favoured with visits to Reynolds' studio. He was also supposed to have witnessed many of the key events of the Revolution, including the trial of Louis XVI in January 1793. However since his name is entered as student at the Royal Academy Schools on 31 December 1792, some of his recollections must be taken with a pinch of salt.

Nonetheless, as the Wellcome drawings show, Masquerier had a precocious talent as a draughtsman. Many of these works are inscribed, including a very accomplished drawing of a faun, which is dated '26 Nov. 1790 / 12 years'. The drawings exhibit a wide range of subject matter including a study of the *Borghese Gladiator* (inscribed: 'J.J. Masquerier / by this I had my ticket for the life'), the *Dying Gaul,* the *Discobolus,* and several highly finished life drawings in coloured chalks. The present study differs from British life drawings of the period, which display a far less doctinaire approach to the figure (see for example cats.58 and 60). Here, as the unfinished legs indicate, Masquerier clearly began with a precise outline, before proceeding to work on the figure, with chalk and stump, to produce a highly finished drawing which pays close attention to the musculature of the figure.   M.P.

Male nude   53
WILLIAM MULREADY
(Co. Clare 1787 - London 1863)
Black chalk on paper; 61 x 50.8 cm
c.1806-7

PROVENANCE: Purchased at the artist's sale, Christie's 28-30.4.1864

The Board of Trustees, Victoria and Albert Museum, London

This drawing is one of a large collection of academic studies by William Mulready, spanning the period of his studentship in the Royal Academy Schools to his time as Visitor there and at the South Kensington Schools in the early 1860s. Collectively they form possibly the most comprehensive record of a British artist's activity in the Life Class over more than half a century. This work probably dates from around 1806-7 – Mulready's early years in the Royal Academy Life School. In 1806 Mulready was awarded a Silver Medal for drawing, and by 1807

was singled out by George Farington for his ability to draw the human figure: 'Mulready a young man Twenty one or two years of age is reckoned to draw the best, but sets Himself high upon it as if He had done His business' (Farington, VIII, p.3142). Farington noted at the same time that Henry Tresham (1751-1814), who was then a Visitor in the Life Schools, thought that he had never seen 'so many good drawings in the Academy at one time before' (ibid.). Indeed, among the students then attending the Life Class were David Wilkie, Benjamin Robert Haydon, and Constable. This drawing is, in fact, quite similar to several male life drawings by Constable of the period 1807-08, and may well be based on the same model (Parris et al., 1976, cats. 85 and 86).   M.P.

Two male nudes   (COL PLATE XIII)   54
WILLIAM ETTY (York 1787 - 1849)
Red chalk on paper; 50.2 x 33.3 cm
? c.1816-22

PROVENANCE: Purchased 1907
LITERATURE: Farr, 1958, no.323

Nottingham Castle Museum and Art Gallery

The use of two or more models posed together in the Life Class was not uncommon. There is, for example, a life drawing by Turner, dating from c.1792-4, in the Victoria and Albert Museum (9262), which shows two male nudes posed in combat. Constable (see cat.26) and Etty, both used models in groups when they were Visitors at the Royal Academy in the 1830s. Maclise, then a student, recalled: 'I have known him [Etty] set three or four models together. Now it was a group of Graces; now a composition of two or three gladiators. Sometimes a dark man or a tawney female was introduced, for a picturesque contrast with a fair form of the same sex' (Gilchrist, 1855, vol.2, p.57). This drawing, executed entirely in red chalk, is unusual in Etty's *oeuvre,* as most of the artist's surviving drawings are in pencil, black chalk, watercolour, or a

combination of all three media. The use of red chalk, which was more common in continental academies, together with the formal, academic attitudes of the two posed models, which does not seem to relate to a specific historical composition – as was the norm in England – raises the possibility that this drawing was made by Etty on the Continent rather than at the Royal Academy Schools.   M.P.

Female nude, standing on a ledge   55

LOUIS CHÉRON (Paris 1660 - London 1725)

Black chalk, heightened with white, on grey paper;
61.1 x 44.6 cm
c.1720-24

PROVENANCE: From an album of drawings by Chéron assembled by James, 10th Earl of Derby; by family descent to Edward, 18th Earl of Derby; bought by the British Museum at the sale of his collection, Christie's (London, 19.10.1953, lot 1)

EXHIBITED: British Museum 1987 (174)

LITERATURE: Croft Murray and Hulton 1960, p.278, no.5 (71); Stainton and White 1987, p.219, no.174

The Trustees of the British Museum, London

The drawing is one of a group of ten studies of the nude female model executed by Chéron at the first St. Martin's Lane Academy between 1720 and 1724 (Croft-Murray and Hulton, 1960, p.278 nos. 66-73, and p.280 nos. 91-92; figs. 10 and 16). It is contemporary with a drawing executed by Hogarth at the same Academy (cat.56). The female model had been used in artists' studios since the Renaissance. They were apparently employed occasionally at some Italian and German academies from an early date, but the regular study of the female nude at

academies was not common practice until the 19th century. During the previous 150 years the nude female model was not used at the *Académie Royale de Peinture et de Sculpture* in Paris, nor at the French Academy in Rome. This fact perhaps explains why Chéron, who was educated there, seems ill at ease when drawing from the female model. In England, the nude female model was employed at the Academy of c.1673 (ill.2), but it was not until 1720, when the first St. Martin's Lane Academy was established, that the study of the female nude became an integral part of the academic curriculum.   I.B.

Female nude seated   56

WILLIAM HOGARTH (London 1697-1764)

Black chalk heightened with white on grey paper;
48.6 x 28.7 cm
c.1720-24

PROVENANCE: Colnaghi

EXHIBITED: British Museum 1987 (197)

LITERATURE: Stainton and White 1987, no.197

The Trustees of the British Museum, London

This drawing was probably executed at the first St. Martin's Lane Academy and is contemporary with a group of ten drawings of the nude female model by Chéron (Croft-Murray and Hulton, 1960, p.278, nos. 66-73, and p.280, nos. 91-92; no.62 and ills. 10 and 16). The model is possibly the same, but while Hogarth gave her a realistic face, Chéron used a 'mask', a stereotyped face ultimately derived from Raphael (ill.9). The habit of using a 'mask' for the female model is also seen in drawing books (ill.15). A comparison between Hogarth's and Chéron's female nudes of the early 1720s shows how a mature artist (Chéron) could find himself less at ease than a young student (Hogarth) with the rendering of the living model. In fact, Chéron, who had attended the *Académie Royale de Peinture et de Sculpture* in Paris and the French Academy in

Female nude, seated (see cat.57)

Rome, was not trained in drawing from the living female body and could not avoid observing the female body through the eyes of Old Masters he had copied in Rome. Hogarth's approach was free from such prejudices and his hand, softer and more sensuous than Chéron's, was sympathetic to the rendering of female forms. Yet his ability as a draughtsman, his observation of the living model and his search for the rendering of the flesh and skin was still in its infancy. It took Hogarth another decade to reform the language of the female body and to produce such a masterpice as his *Female nude* of *c.*1735 (ill.17), which visually announces ideas that the artist fully developed in his *Analysis of Beauty* of 1753 (cat.37).   I.B.

Female nude, seated   57

ALLAN RAMSAY (Edinburgh 1713 - Dover 1784)

Red chalk on paper; 35.5 x 26.5 cm
*c.*1755-59

PROVENANCE: McEwan Gallery; John North

Private Collection, Canada

This red chalk drawing, which is among the most attractive of the artist's life drawings, probably dates from the second half of the 1750s, and may have been made either in Italy, or in the Academy in St. Martin's Lane. While Ramsay's drawing style during his first Italian sojourn (1736-8) was similar to the precise draughtsmanship of Pompeo Batoni (1708-87), whose studies have been mistaken for Ramsay's own (see Kenwood, 1982, p.84 ff.), later studies, such as this drawing, exhibit a much freer handling, and heavier hatching, which is closer to contemporary French draughtsmanship (see also cat.51).

I am grateful to Alastair Smart for his help in cataloguing this work.   M.P.

Female nude, reclining   58

JAMES BARRY (Cork 1741 - London 1806)

Pen and brown ink, with black chalk, heightened with white chalk on brown paper; 31.9 x 52.4 cm
Inscribed lower right: *Jas. Barry Delt*

PROVENANCE: Bought A.P. Oppé, May 1922; by descent

EXHIBITED: Tate Gallery 1983 (83)

LITERATURE: Pressly 1981, cat.91, p.258; Pressly 1983, cat.83, pp.138-9

Private Collection

There are, altogether, 18 known life drawings by James Barry, five of which, including this one, are from the female model. Barry, who arrived in London from Dublin in 1763, seems to have studied casts at the Duke of Richmond's sculpture gallery, and, we may assume, also drew from the life at the St. Martin's Lane Academy. In 1765 he left for Italy, and on his way drew from the life at the *Académie de Saint-Luc* in Paris (Pressly, 1981, p.7). On his arrival in Rome Barry drew from classical statuary and attended life drawing classes at the French Academy and *Accademia del Nudo*. He returned to England in 1770, and on 2 November 1772 was made an Associate Royal Academician. In February 1773 he was elected a full Academician. From 1774 until his expulsion from the Academy in 1799 Barry was a frequent Visitor in the Life Schools. His own drawing style was, however, very different from the highly-worked studies encouraged in the Academy. Most of his drawings, like this one, are executed in pen and ink over a slight outline in pencil or chalk. Stephen Rigaud recalled: 'Mr. Barry, as soon as he had placed the model, used to go into the Hall and return with a piece of coarse brown or packing paper, and a pen and ink, with which he sketched and shaded the figure, touching up the lights with a piece of the common white chalk used for marking the place where the

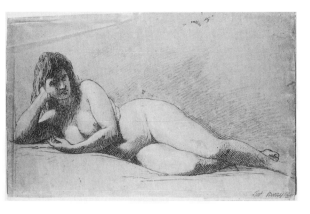

model stands; thus making a bold clever sketch of the figure with coarse materials that cost him nothing' (quoted in Pressly, 1981, p.256). In addition to drawing at the Academy Barry also drew extensively from the model while working on his Society of Arts project (see cat.24). There he was given an allowance of £45 for models, although Barry paid his female models directly as they wished to remain anonymous (op. cit., p.215 no.17).

The drawing exhibited here is notable not only for its rapid pen and ink technique, but also for the sensuousness of the model's attitude. Barry, in his *Inquiry into the Present State of the Arts*, had written apropos the issue of nudity in the human figure: 'a great mind can raise great and virtuous ideas, though he shews all parts of the body in their natural way; whilst the Cheapside prints of the Buck and Quaker Girl, the Charm of the Garter and of the High Wind, are proofs that very lewd ideas might be produced, though little or nothing of the naked be discovered' (see Barry, 1809, vol.2, p.260).   M.P.

Female nude, seated   59

GEORGE ROMNEY
(Dalton-le-Furness 1734 - Kendal 1802)
Black chalk, worked with stump, strengthened with black chalk, and heightened with white, on buff paper; 47.9 x 40.3 cm
c.1773-75

PROVENANCE: Presented by Rev. John Romney, 1818

EXHIBITED: Cambridge, 1977 (4)

LITERATURE: Jaffé, 1977, pp.6-7

Fitzwilliam Museum, Cambridge

This drawing is one of a series of 12 life studies made by Romney during his stay in Rome, 1773-5. It is unusual, in terms of known British 18th-century life drawings, in that it was almost certainly made privately, rather than in the Academy. Romney's son recalled after the artist's death: 'There was at that time a young female of fine form, who lent herself to the artists for hire as a naked model, and by these means supported herself and her mother. Notwithstanding this species of prostitution, it does not appear that her mind was actually corrupt. Her mother always attended her, so that she was never left alone; and as much delicacy and decorum were observed as the nature of the business would admit of. Had the slightest liberty been attempted, it would have been repelled with indignation; so, at least, it was generally understood. Mr Romney availed himself of so favourable an opportunity for studying the nude and made many sketches from her; thus he acquired an accurate knowledge of the female form in all its diversities of attitude' (Romney 1830, p.97). In 1809, Romney's patron William Hayley had felt compelled to make a similar point about Romney's Roman model, noting that 'her modesty and discretion were so great, that he never beheld her except in the presence of her mother'. (Hayley, 1809, p.57).

Despite John Romney's and Hayley's stress on the academic nature of the exercise and their concern with the observation of propriety, these private studies are remarkable for their candidness. Here, for example, the model lounges on a couch, proffering her breast, while supported by cushions and drapery. As Patricia Jaffé has noted, the pose of the model has much in common with the sensuality of Boucher's female nudes.   M.P.

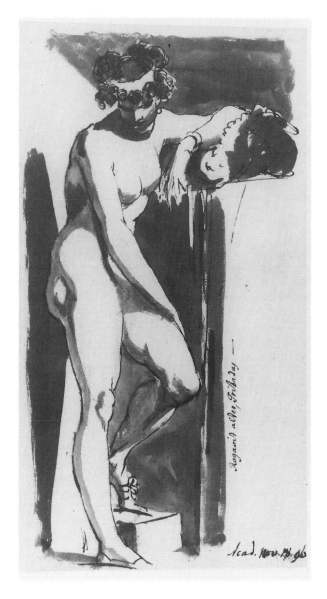

Female nude, standing, from front　60a

HENRY FUSELI (Zurich 1741 - London 1825)

Pen, ink and wash on paper; 20 x 11 cm
Inscribed: *Rogavit alter, Tribadas* and *Acad. Nov. 18 96*

PROVENANCE: Presented by E. Peter Jones, Esq.

LITERATURE: Ziff, vol.1, 1973, no.1127

The Trustees of the British Museum, London

Female Nude, standing, from rear　60b

Pen, ink, and wash on paper
Inscribed: τι δε τις; τι δ' 8τις; Σχιας ουαρ αυϑρωπος
and *Acad. Nov. 17. 96*

PROVENANCE: Presented by E. Peter Jones, Esq.

LITERATURE: Ziff, vol.1, 1973 (no.1128)

The Trustees of the British Museum, London

Henry Fuseli first visited London in 1764, although his artistic training did not really begin in earnest until his Italian sojourn from 1770 to 1778. In 1788 he became Associate Royal Academician, and a full Academician two years later in 1790. These two drawings are dated by the artist to 17th and 18th November 1796. In their reliance on line and wash, rather than on careful execution in chalks, they are reminiscent of the life-drawings of James Barry (see cat.58), although Fuseli did not possess Barry's control of line. Fuseli drew the figure frequently, although usually his studies were based on his own imagination, rather than on the living model. Several other life drawings of the female model, all in a combination of pen and ink, and wash, do however exist, including one in the British Museum dated to 1800 (Ziff, 1973, vol.1, no.1453) and two in Basle (Ziff, 1973, vol.1, nos. 1126 and 1454), the second of which is closely related to the two drawings shown here.

Fuseli was a frequent Visitor at the Royal Academy Schools during the 1790s, although his greatest impact on the teaching of life-drawing occurred when he was appointed Keeper in 1804. His impact was felt on a whole generation of artists including Wilkie, Mulready, Constable, and Haydon. Fuseli had a reputation for leaving students to their own devices, although an essay in the *Polytechnic Journal* of 1840, presented a somewhat different picture: 'Boldness of outline and vigour of execution were sure to elicit his approbation. He loved a decision of style as he hated what he called "a neegling tooch". Woe to the poor student who depended on his elaborate finishing. After having been a week or ten days working up his drawing with the softest chalk, stumping, dotting, stippling until he had nearly worn his eyes out, the Keeper would stealthily come behind him, and looking over this shoulder would grasp the porte-crayon, and, standing at arms length from the drawing, would give so terrific a score as to cut through the paper and leave a distinct outline on the board beneath; and then would say, by way of encouragement to future exertion, "There, Saar, there, you should have a boldness of handling and a greater fwreedom of tooch"'. (Whitley, 1928, vol.2, p.82). For a comparison of the present drawings with one in a sketch book by Turner, see cat.73a.　　M.P

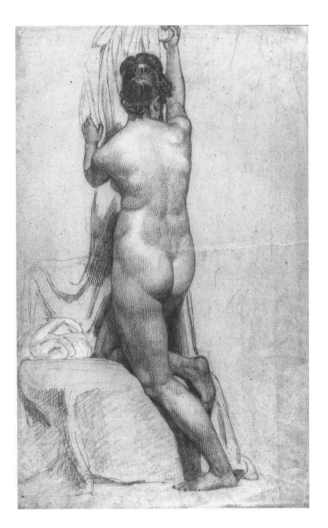

Female nude, seated   61

JOHN CONSTABLE
(East Bergholt 1776 - London 1837)
Black chalk and pencil, heightened with white, on paper;
38 x 27.7 cm
Inscribed by Hugh Golding Constable, grandson of the artist:
'By J.C.'
c.1807-8

PROVENANCE: By descent from the artist

Richard Constable

The strong hatching employed by Constable in this work is characteristic of a group of nine drawings ascribed by Shirley to around 1808 (Shirley, 1933, pp.216-7). In all he listed a total of 33 life drawings by Constable over the period c.1800 to 1820, although this drawing is not included. The precise dating of Constable's life drawings is fraught with difficulty, not because of a shortage of known works – we have more drawings by Constable than by many of his contemporaries – but because there is an inevitable tendency to group works around those dates for which we have documentary evidence that Constable was working from the life. On 16 November 1807, for example, Farington noted that Constable 'attends the Life Academy every evening' (Farington, VIII, p.3142), while in the summer of 1808 he was recorded painting from the life with Wilkie there (see cat.14). In 1811 he dated a female life drawing on 10 December (Shirley, 1933, no.15), and again in February and August 1820 (op. cit., nos. 26 and 29). This work could plausibly have been made around 1807. A comparison with cat.26 reveals that Constable had softened the outline of his figures in favour of a more generalised attention to the play of light and shade across the figure.   M.P.

Female nude, standing   62

JOSHUA CRISTALL (Camborne 1768 - London 1847)
Black chalk, with traces of white, on paper; 53.3 x 33.4 cm
c.1820

PROVENANCE: Mrs George Norman, Bath; bequeathed to Victoria Art Gallery, 1939

The Victoria Art Gallery, Bath City Council

This drawing is one of a group of life-studies which were included in the six lots of drawings in the artist's studio sale from 11-13 April 1848 (232-3 and 235-8). Cristall entered the Royal Academy Schools on 3 November 1792 (Hutchison, 1962, p.153), although the style and accomplished nature of many of the drawings in the Victoria Art Gallery, including this one, suggest they were executed at a later date. One clue to the dating of this drawing however is its close similarity to a series of full-length oil-studies of the female model by William Etty (for example, Phillips, 11 November 1980, lot 59), which in turn relate to the central figure in Etty's *Candaules, King of Lydia, showing his wife by stealth to Gyges, one of his Ministers: As she goes to Bed* (Tate Gallery). This painting was exhibited by Etty at the Royal Academy in 1830. As this work is similar to drawings made by Etty in the early to mid-1820s, it is possible that it was made at the Academy just prior to Cristall's departure for Herefordshire in 1822 – especially as he did not return to London until June 1841, when he moved to Hampstead. The naked human figure often featured in Cristall's work, especially during his years in London, and surviving drawings indicate that he frequently made chalk and pencil studies for his finished pictures (Cristall, 1975, pp.116-18).   M.P.

Female nude, seated (COL PLATE XIV) **63**

Sir DAVID WILKIE (Cults, Fifeshire 1785 - Gibraltar 1841)

Red and black chalks, heightened with white, on buff paper;
31.9 x 27 cm
*c.*1833

PROVENANCE: P.M. Turner; purchased 1942

EXHIBITED: Oxford Art Club 1935 (18); Rembrandt Gallery
1939 (31); St. Andrews and Aberdeen 1985 (45)

LITERATURE: Oxford and London, 1985, p.50

The Ashmolean Museum, Oxford

This drawing, which has been dated to the early 1830s (Oxford
and London, 1985, p.50), is among the latest works in the
exhibition. In addition to demonstrating the development in
the artist's style towards a more linear approach to the figure,
founded on his admiration of Rubens, the drawing also reveals
a less idealised approach towards the depiction of the model,
which can be observed in other artists during this period –
notably Etty and Mulready. Indeed there are stylistic and
formal similarities between this drawing and studies of the
female model by Mulready of the same period (see for example
Rorimer, 1972, nos. 30 and 31). Wilkie, like Mulready,
although by profession principally a *genre* painter, had an
abiding interest in drawing the human figure. Nonetheless the
Redgraves, somewhat unfairly, stated that 'although he drew
readily and imitated his model well, he never was a good
draughtsman, and when he attempted beauty his defects
became apparent' (Redgrave, 1947, p.317). Wilkie evidently
drew from the naked model in his studio as well as the
Academy, as a candid drawing in the British Museum, of a
female nude climbing a ladder holding a paint-pot indicates
(ill.11). It is perhaps worth noting in the context of this
drawing that Wilkie's very absorption in the study of
individuals in common-place surroundings and in everyday
situations, must have had a bearing on the anti-academic bias
of his later life drawings. M.P.

Puggs Graces etched from his original daubing **64**

PAUL SANDBY (Nottingham 1725 - Windsor 1798)

Engraving; 22.3 x 17.2 cm
Inscribed: *Puggs GRACES Etched from his ORIGINAL Daubing*
1753

LITERATURE: Stephens and Hawkins 1877, no.3242; Paulson,
1971, vol.2, pp.144-52, repr.

The Trustees of the British Museum, London

In November 1753 Hogarth published the *Analysis of Beauty*,
in which he had, among other things, attacked the burgeoning
desire among his fellow artists for an Academy shaped along
continental lines. In December Paul Sandby, who was one of
the group who opposed Hogarth, published eight etchings,
including *Puggs Graces*, which were intended to undermine
Hogarth's position. Sandby, who had recently completed his
work on the Survey of Scotland, was, by early 1753 holding life
drawing classes with his brother Thomas (1723-98) in their
house in Poultney Street. An invitation card, dated 26
February survives, and is inscribed: 'To Sit or Sketch a figure
here / We'll Study hard from Six till Nine / And then attack
cold Beef and Wine...' (quoted in Paulson, 1971, vol.2 p.149).
In *Puggs Graces* Hogarth, his legs shown to resemble those of
his own pug-dog, is depicted painting from three grotesque
female models representing a travesty of the three Graces –
who traditionally represent beauty, charm and grace. In the
right foreground is a book in which Hogarth purportedly gives
'Reasons against a Publick Academy', the principal one ('No
Salary') being that Hogarth had objected to the suggestion put
forward of having salaried professors. The large man gesturing
towards the Graces is intended to represent Hogarth's friend,
Dr. Benjamin Hoadly. M.P.

A Life Class **65**

S.F. RAVENET, after John Hamilton Mortimer
(Eastbourne 1741 - London 1779)

Line engraving by S.F. Ravenet; 51 x 42.5 cm
Inscribed: *John Mortimer Pinxit, S.F. Ravenet Sculpsit. Published
November 1st 1771 by John Boydell, Engraver, Cheapside, London*

EXHIBITED: Proof print exhibited R.A., 1771 (154)

LITERATURE: Sunderland, 1986, pp.141-2, no.49

Wellcome Institute Library, London

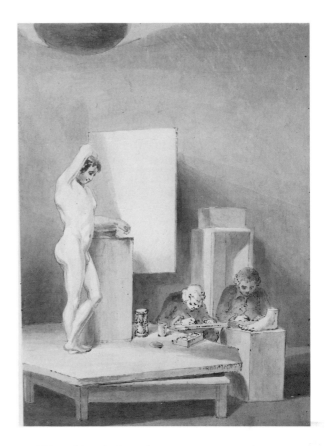

As Sunderland has noted, this engraving formed the frontispiece to the second volume of John Boydell's *A Collection of Prints*, published in 1772, although it is not known whether it was designed specifically for this purpose. A 'Drawing from the Painting by Mortimer' had already been exhibited in Boydell's Exhibition in 'Ford's Great Room in the Haymarket' in 1770 (22) (Sunderland, 1986, cat.49b). Of this engraving Sunderland states: 'The standing nude male model has a hairstyle which was fashionable c.1759-60. The model is being drawn and painted in a room with a curved wall, faced with an entablature of plain triglyths and metopes supported by doric pilasters. In the foreground a doric column is swathed by a curtain drape', (Sunderland, 1986, 142). A copy in grisaille of Mortimer's engraving by an unknown artist (Private Collection, USA) is inscribed on the back of the stretcher: 'JOHAN ZOFFANY RA. ST. MARTIN'S LANE ACADEMY 1762' (Sunderland, 1986, cat.49a). Sunderland notes that the academy shown by Mortimer is probably imaginary. The grand surroundings suggest a continental academy rather than a British one – although Mortimer never travelled abroad. (For discussion of a putative painting of the St. Martin's Lane Academy see cat.4). M.P.

A Life Class 66

JOHN THOMAS SMITH,
attributed to (London 1766 - 1833)

Pen and ink, and brown wash on paper; 20.4 x 15.2 cm
? c.1788-91

PROVENANCE: L.G. Duke

Private Collection

This drawing, which is ascribed to John Thomas Smith, has stylistic similarities to other known works by the artist (for example a pen and wash portrait of James Boswell, Sotheby's 19 July 1979, lot 100). Nothing, however, is known about the circumstances in which it was produced. Smith, who is best known for his work as an antiquarian, and his biography of Joseph Nollekens (see cat.36) was not a pupil at the Royal Academy Schools. He trained in Nolleken's studio from 1778

to 1781, although his subsequent artistic work was as a topographical draughtsman. This drawing does not seem to depict the Royal Academy Schools, but a much smaller class for amateurs rather than for aspiring professionals. The two seated men, for example, appear to be drawing from the cast of a foot, although they are in the presence of the living model – whereas life drawing and drawing from the Antique usually took place in separate rooms. It is known that Smith worked as a drawing master in Edmonton in the late 1780s and early '90s, which raises the possibility that this drawing was done at that time. Nonetheless, it was not, as far as it is known, the general practice to draw from the living model at such establishments. M.P.

A Dutch Academy 67

THOMAS ROWLANDSON (London 1756-1827)

Pencil, pen and ink, and watercolour; 18.2 x 28.5 cm
c.1792

PROVENANCE: Bought by the present owner, Christie's 10.7.1990, lot 97

LITERATURE: Grego 1880, I, pp.306-7; George, 1938, vol.6, no.8195; Wark, 1975, p.53

ENGRAVED: T. Rowlandson, March 1792

Katrin Bellinger

The opposition of Dutch conceptions of the human figure to an Italianate or classical ideal was well-established by the end of the 18th century, it being commonplace to admire Rembrandt's handling whilst deploring his inability to infuse beauty into the female form. Even by the late-19th century, Joseph Grego noted how this drawing 'represents, as the title describes, the interior of a drawing school in Holland; just as one may be found there to this day' (Grego, 1880, vol.1, p.306-7). The print after Rowlandson's watercolour, *The Dutch Academy*, was published in 1792 (George, no.8195). It is one of a number of satirical

views of the Life Class produced by Rowlandson (George, no.9785 and no.14953), although it is the only one which does not directly refer to the Royal Academy Schools. According to George, Rowlandson's print of the Life Class at the Royal Academy, which was published in 1801 (George, no.9785), was intended as a companion, or corrective, to this work, although it could be argued that its intention was also to satirise, as the female model's provocative pose and the presence of a bottle and glass on the podium indicate. A far more straightforward depiction by Rowlandson of the Academy's Life Class appeared in Ackermann's *Microcosm of London* in 1808 (vol.1, opp. p.9), where students are shown seated in an orderly manner diligently drawing from a male model – whose back is turned to the viewer. Rowlandson's own behaviour as a student in the Academy Schools (he enrolled as a student there on 6 November 1772 [Hutchison, 1962, p.138]) had not always been distinguished by earnest application, as his friend Henry Angelo recalled: 'The latter once gave great offence, by carrying a pea-shooter into the life academy, and, whilst old Moser was adjusting the female model, and had just directed her contour, Rowlandson let fly a pea, which making her start, she threw herself entirely out of position, and interrupted the gravity of the study for the whole evening. For this offence, Master Rowlandson went near to getting himself expelled' (Angelo, 1904, vol.1, p.202). Versions of this drawing exist in the Widener and Morris Saffron collections in the United States (see Wark, 1975, p.53).   M.P.

A Meeting of Connoisseurs   (COL PLATE XV)   68

JOHN BOYNE (Co. Down 1750-? 1810)

Watercolour; 41.3 x 55.6 cm
*c.*1807

PROVENANCE: William Smith Gift

EXHIBITED: Tokyo, 1987/88

LITERATURE: Williams, 1952, vol.1, p.146, vol.2, fig.237

The Board of Trustees, Victoria and Albert Museum, London

A Meeting of Connoisseurs features a group of men and an artist in a studio looking at a black model posed with a broom. The subject is treated satirically, perhaps because at the time a black model as an embodiment of the classical ideal of physical perfection would have been considered unusual. Nonetheless, several years later, on 18 August 1810 Farington recorded in his diary a black sailor who had sat to several artists including Thomas Lawrence 'who thought Him the finest figure He had ever seen, combining the character & perfection of many Antique Statues. "When His arm was suspended it appeared like that of the Antinous; when contracted for exertion

it was like the Farnese Hercules"' (Farington, X, 3713). This is probably the same model whom Haydon records drawing from frequently the same year (see Elwin, 1950, p.123). There are quite a number of drawings by Haydon of a black model in the British Museum, one of which is inscribed: 'Wilson the Black Nov. 1 1810' (1881-7-9-523). In 1818 the *Annals of the Fine Arts* (VII, 481), in an attack on the reactionary behaviour of the Royal Academy stated: 'When Wilson the Negro was discovered, Haydon, Chantry, Westmacott, and Lawrence all moulded him for their own peculiar studies, and thereby presented his wonderful form. The Academy never moulded him for the use of their students. – Was this not liberal?' The 'moulding' referred to above may relate to Haydon's decision to take a cast from Wilson's body, an operation which nearly cost the model his life (see Elwin, 1950, pp.123-4). In addition to Haydon's drawings of Wilson, Benjamin West is recorded to have made a study of him (von Erffa and Staley, 1986, cat.495). A study of a black model by Etty, which can also be identified as Wilson, was recently sold at auction (Sotheby's 24.10.1984, lot 275).   M.P.

Figg the Gladiator   69

JONATHAN RICHARDSON THE ELDER
(London 1665 ?-1745)

Black and white chalks on blue paper; 29 x 22.5 cm
Inscribed in ink beneath upper margin by Jonathan Richardson the Younger: *Figg the Gladiator ad Vivum*; in red chalk lower left corner; *1714* in black chalk lower right corner.
1714

PROVENANCE: Randall Davies: Sir Hugh Walpole (no.59 in the dispersal of the Walpole collection at the Leicester Galleries, 1945); bought by the Ashmolean Museum (Hope Collection), 1945.

EXHIBITED: British Museum, 1987 (182)

LITERATURE: Brown, 1982, no.1532; Brown, 1983, no.20; Stainton and White, 1987, p.228, no.182

The Ashmolean Museum, Oxford

This drawing was executed by the artist, from the life, in 1714. At that time Richardson was one of the directors of the Academy in Great Queen Street (Bignamini 1988B, 3) and was about to publish the first of his essays on art, *The Theory of Painting* of 1715. It is highly probable that this portrait of James Figg (d.1734) was executed at the Academy and that the pugilist was one of the models who sat before the artists in Great Queen Street (Stainton and White, 1987, p.228, no.182), was an ideal

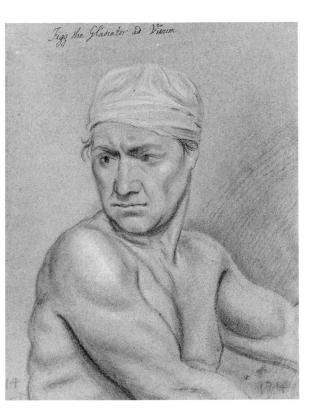

model for the Life Class. He possibly also posed before artists attending the first St. Martin's Lane Academy in 1720-24. Yet to identify him as the sitter in specific life drawings is not really possible. Facial similarities with the model in certain drawings by Chéron (cats. 43 and 49) can however be noticed.　　I.B.

John Malin　　70
THOMAS BANKS (London 1735-1805)
Black and red chalks, heightened with white, on paper laid on canvas; 48.5 x 37 cm
c.1768-69

PROVENANCE: Possibly presented to the Royal Academy by the artist

EXHIBITED: Royal Academy, 1771 (6); 1963 (76)

LITERATURE: Hutchison, 1968, repr. pl.9

Royal Academy of Arts, London

As an inscription on the back states, 'this fine drawing ... is a portrait of John Malin the first porter and model at the Royal Academy, which posts he had filled at the Academy in Peter House St. Martin's Lane from which the Royal Academy emanated'. Malin's wife, Elizabeth was also appointed first 'Sweeper', or caretaker, at the Royal Academy. Article XV of the Instrument of Foundation of the Royal Academy, dated 10 December 1768, stated: 'There shall be a Porter of the Royal Academy, whose sallary shall be twenty-five pounds a year; he shall have a room in the Royal Academy, and receive his orders from the Keeper, or Secretary'. (Hutchison, 1968, p.212). Malin was appointed to the position of porter on 17 December 1768. Evidently he had been employed in the St. Martin's Lane Academy, and was simply transferred, alongside the benches, casts, and other paraphernalia to the new Academy (see Hutchison, 1968, p.48). He died early in 1769, whereupon the Academy agreed to pay funeral expenses of £6 2s 2d, owing to his 'long and faithful services' (see Royal Academy Council Minutes, vol.1, p.20). There is also a miniature of Malin by Ozias Humphrey in the Royal

Collection. At least two of Malin's successors also worked in the capacity of model as well as porter at the Royal Academy: Charles Cranmer (see cat.34), and Samuel Strowger, who modelled to Haydon, Etty, and Constable (see cat.72), in the early 19th century.　　M.P.

Dionysius Areopagites　　71
JOHN JEHNER after Sir Joshua Reynolds (1723-1792)
Mezzotint engraving; 25.7 x 19.2 cm
Inscribed in ink: *Sir Joshua Reynolds / pinxt J. Jehner fecit,* and below

LITERATURE: Hamilton 1874, p.147; Postle, 1988, p.737, repr.

David Alexander

This mezzotint is based on a lost oil painting by Sir Joshua Reynolds, which employs the features of his favourite model, George White. Reynolds came across White in 1770, after he had been confined with a fever in St. George's Hospital, which was then administered by John Hunter. Afterwards he went to live with William Hunter in his house in Windmill Street, where he was used by Hunter in demonstrations to medical students. Although he was clearly quite old, White apparently still had a marvellous physique not least because of a life spent in laying paving slabs. It was for this reason, rather than his venerable features, that he was also used as a model in the Royal Academy Schools. During the early 1770s, when he was at the height of his popularity, White featured in subject pictures by a number of prominent artists including Zoffany, John Russell, West, and Reynolds, who also used him as the central figure in *Ugolino and his Children in the Dungeon* (Lord Sackville). In this work Reynolds attempted to produce a 'companion' to the paintings of patriarchs by old masters such as Carracci, Ribera and Domenico Fetti (see Postle, 1988, pp.735-6). The title of the mezzotint, which is engraved on a

state of the print in the British Museum (1833-7-15-63), may well, as with other similar works by the artist, have been invented by Jehner rather than by Reynolds himself.   M.P.

Guardsman Higgins   72

WILLIAM ETTY

Oil on board; 66.6 x 51.3 cm
A label on the back states: *The Guardsman Higgins, William Etty's favourite Male Model*
c.1830

PROVENANCE: Bought, at Etty's studio sale, May 1850, by John Mogford; Clayton Cole; Durlacher Brothers, New York; William Doyle Galleries, New York; thence to present owner

The Forbes Magazine Collection, New York

Despite the claim on a label on the back of this picture that Higgins was Etty's favourite model, there is no hard evidence to back up the assertion. Nonetheless Guardsman Higgins' presence in the exhibition may stand for a whole series of soldiers who supplemented their income by modelling privately and at the Royal Academy. Benjamin Robert Haydon, who had more to say about his models than most, placed great emphasis on the qualities of soldiers as models, and made frequent reference to them in his autobiography. Corporal Sammons, who had been in the Peninsular War, he described as 'a living Ilissus' (Elwin, 1950, p.256), while Hodgson, another of his models, who had fought at Waterloo, he described as 'a perfect Achilles', (op. cit., p.257). Naturally soldiers (even more than boxers – see cat.69), made excellent models, not merely because of their good physique but because of their ability to remain still for protracted periods. Perhaps the best known soldier-model in the early-19th century was Samuel Strowger, who began to pose at the Royal Academy in the early-19th century while still in the Life Guards. Strowger, who was painted by Constable, Wilkie, and Etty, was so popular that the Academicians effected his release from the army in 1802 when he became porter and model at the Royal Academy Schools (Beckett, II, p.28).   M.P.

Guardsman Higgins (see cat.72)

Female nude, standing   (COL PLATE XVI)   73a

J.M.W. TURNER (1775-1851)

'Academical' Sketchbook
Pencil, watercolour and bodycolour, on blue paper prepared with a red-brown wash; 21.6 x 14 cm
1796-? 1798

PROVENANCE: Turner Bequest; XLIII f.13

EXHIBITED: Tate Gallery 1989 (5)

LITERATURE: Finberg, 1909, vol.1, p.106; Chumbley and Warrell, 1989, no.5

The Turner Collection, Tate Gallery, London

This study is one of several life drawings in the so-called 'Academical' sketchbook, made by Turner following his admission to the Life Class (the 'Academy of Living Models') in 1792. Turner's first appearance in the Life Class is recorded on 25 June 1792. As, however, it had been agreed by the Council of the Royal Academy in 1769 that 'no Student under the Age of twenty, be admitted to draw after the Female Model, unless he be a married Man', Turner would not have been eligible to draw from the female model until at least April 1795. According to Chumbley and Warrell (1989, p.13) Turner's first drawing from the female model is perhaps contained in the 'Wilson' sketchbook, which he used from 1796. The present sketchbook contains 13 drawings from male and female models both seated and standing and from a variety of angles. All are executed in a combination of watercolour, bodycolour and pencil. The 'Academical' sketchbook is usually dated to 1798, although a comparison between the present study and Henry Fuseli's drawing, dated November 1796 (cat.61), which shows a female model in the exact same pose, and wearing a similar headband, suggests that the studies may have been made at the same time.

Kneeling Academy figure 73c

Life Class (2) Sketchbook
Red Chalk; 18.4 x 7.3 cm

PROVENANCE: Turner Bequest; CCLXXIX(b) f.21

LITERATURE: Finberg, 1909, vol.2, p.890

The Turner Collection, Tate Gallery, London

The drawings in this sketchbook show a number of models, male and female, from a variety of positions. All the drawings are in red-chalk outlines and suggest that Turner was moving around the Life Class making rapid studies. Ruskin, who after the artist's death destroyed a number of Turner's figure drawings which he thought to be indecent, inscribed this sketchbook: 'kept as evidence of the failure of mind only'. M.P.

Life Class at the Royal Academy 73b

Life Class (1) Sketchbook
Pencil; 8.6 x 11.1 cm
c.1832

PROVENANCE: Turner Bequest; CCLXXIX(a) ff.51 verso

LITERATURE: Finberg, 1909, vol.2, pp.887-89; Chumbley and Warrell, 1989 cat.11 repr.; Brown (1990), p.33, repr.

The Turner Collection, Tate Gallery, London

This pencil sketch was almost certainly made during one of Turner's stints as a Visitor in the Life Schools of the Royal Academy during the early 1830s. It is one of three sketches of the Life School contained by Turner in the sketchbook (see also f.20 verso and ff.58 verso, 59), the final one of which is inscribed 'Visitor waiting (?) for the Model'. Although the sketch is relatively indistinct it is possible to pick out the sheet pinned up behind the female model who is probably lying on an adjustable bench of the kind clearly visible in a life drawing by Mulready of a female model in a similar reclining position (illustrated in Rorimer, 1972, p.17, cat.3). The model may be lit by natural light as the opening at the left may be a window. Certainly, there is no evidence of an artificial lamp in the sketch. (For further commentary on Turner's Visitorship see cat.32).

IV   Anatomy

This section consists of oil paintings, drawings, prints, as well as an anatomical skeleton and two écorché figures, and is designed to illustrate the evolving role of anatomy from the early-18th to the early-19th century, in relation to the study of the model. In England, as opposed to countries like Italy or Holland, there was very little contact between artists and anatomists before 1720. Some British artists who visited Italy from the early-17th century, such as Inigo Jones, did however make anatomical drawings (see Howarth, 1985, p.42, nos. 43-44). Those foreign artists, in turn, who settled in England usually had a knowledge of anatomy. And, it may be presumed, anatomy was already part of the curriculum in academies established in England in the late-17th century. (An anatomical drawing, based on an engraving, which was probably executed in the Academy of c.1673, is to be found in an album of drawings at Dulwich College, London). For the most part, artists depended for their knowledge of anatomy on prints and drawing books, although the active interest in the arts of surgeons like William Patch and William Cowper, fostered a closer relationship between practising artists and anatomists. Crucial to the developing cooperation between artists and anatomists was the establishment of an uninterrupted series of academies in England from 1711 onwards, and the practical demonstrations by anatomists such as William Cheselden, William Hunter, and in the early-19th century, Sir Charles Bell. Finally in the drawings of Haydon and his School, the increasing primacy of anatomy over and above the study of the Antique is explored.

Colour Plate XVIII   JOHAN ZOFFANY *Dr. William Hunter lecturing at the Royal Academy*, c.1772
Royal College of Physicians, London (cat.75)

Colour Plate II – p.38

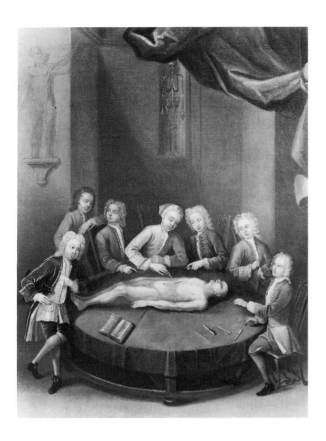

William Cheselden giving an Anatomical Demonstration

74

(COL PLATE XVII)

BRITISH SCHOOL

Oil on canvas; 75.2 x 58 cm
c.1733-35

PROVENANCE: Bought from Eric Waller, Sweden

Wellcome Institute Library, London

This work was painted by an artist of the British School in the early 1730s. Some of the original paint has become worn, especially on the right half of the canvas, and the worn parts have been overpainted, or strengthened, but only following the original tracings. The figure in the centre is reputed to be William Cheselden (1688-1752; see Cope, 1953, Russell, 1954, Bignamini 1988B, 4, and Kemp, f). A pupil of William Cowper, the famous anatomist and member of the club of the Virtuosi of St. Luke (Dumaitre, 1982; Bignamini, 1988B, 1), Cheselden subscribed to the first St. Martin's Lane Academy in 1720. By then he had made a name with his *Anatomy of the Humane Body* of 1713. In the spring of 1721 Cheselden gave a course of lectures on human and comparative anatomy in Crane Court, Fleet Street. This was chiefly designed for a non-medical audience (see the advertisement in *Daily Currant*, 21 March 1721). It is probable that artists of the first St. Martin's Lane Academy attended his lectures and that they, and other artists, attended anatomical demonstrations given by Cheselden and other anatomists in London. The style of the painting is close to that of informal portraitists of the early 1730s produced by artists-members of the Rose and Crown Club, an art club which stimulated the rise and development of the conversation piece in England (Bignamini, 1988B, 2). The date of execution might coincide with the publication of Cheselden's *Osteographia* in 1733. (The anatomy theatre shown is not sufficiently distinct to identify it with a specific theatre). It is perhaps the theatre of the Barber-Surgeons' Company designed by Inigo Jones, built in 1636 near the present site of the Barbican and demolished in 1784. Hogarth may have had the same scene in mind when he

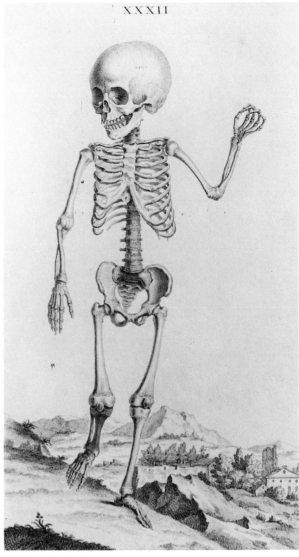

Fig.5   WILLIAM CHESELDEN, *Osteographia*, 1733, pl.XXXII
By permission of the British Library

designed *The Reward of Cruelty* for his *Four Stages of Cruelty* of 1751. The sitters, too, are not described sufficiently so as to identify them with specific persons. The same applies to the écorché, but the book opened at a page illustrated with a human skeleton is more telling. The artful pose is similar to that of the skeleton illustrated at plate XXXII of Cheselden's *Osteographia* of 1733 (fig.5).

I am grateful to William Schupbach for his assistance in cataloguing this work.   I.B.

90 and 91) and a skeleton. These three principal subjects of the anatomist's lecture are, interestingly, illustrated in *The Universal Magazine* of Sept. 1748 (pl. facing p.97 and fig.6), where a surgeon (central figure) points to a skeleton, an écorché and a male nude figure standing. An examination of illustrations reproduced in the magazine from July 1748 to June 1751 would suggest that the plate was engraved by Charles Grignion possibly after an original design by Hubert Gravelot, whose designs were engraved and published in England for many years after his return to France (Hammelmann, 1975, pp.38-46). Grignion was a member of the second St. Martin's Lane Academy from the mid-1750s to the late 1760s (Bignamini 1988B, 5). Zoffany, too, attended the Academy after his arrival in London in 1760. It is possible that Zoffany had Grignion's engraving in mind when he produced his own painting of an anatomy lecture, although it should also be stressed that the similarity between the two images ultimately springs from the fact that they both depict a scene which represents the norm in contemporary anatomical demonstration.   I.B.

Dr. William Hunter lecturing at The Royal Academy   75

(COL PLATE XVIII)

JOHAN ZOFFANY

(Frankfurt-am-Main 1733 - London 1810)

Oil on canvas; 77.5x103.5cm. Oval
Inscribed on wooden label attached to the frame: *William Hunter, M.D. / Lecturing at the Royal Academy / Zoffany R.A. / Bequeathed by Dr M. Baillie. 1823*
c.1772

PROVENANCE: Presumably by family descent to Hunter's nephew and heir Dr. Matthew Baillie (1761-1823), presented by Mrs Baillie his wife, 1825

EXHIBITED: Washington 1976 (360); National Portrait Gallery 1977 (75); Glasgow 1990

LITERATURE: Manners and Williamson, 1920, p.226; Wolstenhome and Piper, 1964, p.232; Kemp, 1975, pp.14-19; Webster, 1977, no.75

Royal College of Physicians, London

The painting shows Dr. William Hunter (cat.77) in his capacity as Professor of Anatomy at the Royal Academy. Apart from Sir Joshua Reynolds, who is seated in the centre holding his ear trumpet (also in cat. no.5), no member of the audience has been identified. To illustrate the subject of his lecture, Hunter makes use of the living model, an écorché figure (see cats. 5, 89,

Fig.6 Anon *A Surgery with a Representation and Explication of the Chirurgical Instruments. The Universal Magazine*, September 1748, facing p.97

John Patch Sr.   76

WILLIAM GANDY (c.1655 - Exeter 1729)

Oil on canvas; 120x81.5cm.
Originally there was an inscription, dated 1717, written by Dr William Musgrave, which, according to Delpratt Harris (1922, p.26), rested between the canvas and the frame and took the form of an eulogy in Latin and Greek in which Patch is described as 'proved as an anatomist and skilful as a surgeon,' and went on to remind the reader that the painting was 'a memorial of friendship,' for Gandy, a grateful patient of Patch.

PROVENANCE: By family descent to John Gandy, son of William, who bequeathed it to the Hospital, 1783

LITERATURE: Delpratt Harris 1922, p.26; Morris 1925, p.149; Russell 1976, p.40

The Trustees of the Royal Devon and Exeter Hospitals

The portrait, 'a memorial of friendship', was painted long before John Patch (1691-1746) joined the staff of the City Hospital. Patch was the father of the surgeon John Patch Jr. (1723-87) and of the painter Thomas Patch (1725-82). Patch, who studied medicine in Paris introduced lithotomy as a surgical operation into the West of England, was appointed surgeon to the Workhouse, later the City Hospital, in 1718, and was one of the five surgeons appointed to the staff of the Exter and Devon Hospital at its foundation in 1741. The painting shows the surgeon demonstrating a dissection of the right forearm. This type of portrait was made famous by the frontispiece to Andreas Vesalius' *De Humani corporis fabrica* (Basle 1543). Rembrandt's *Anatomy lesson of Dr. Nicolaes Tulp* of 1632 (The Hague, Mauritshuis), too, is another obvious precendent. More generally, the human hand had theological and philosophical implications from the time of Aristotle and Galen (Schupbach, 1982, pp.57-65). Its primary purpose is to grip, and it was regarded as the instrument of human civilization *par excellence*. The portrait of Patch is particularly interesting because new elements are added to the traditional iconography of the anatomist's portrait. Gandy and Patch, who were familiar with the symbology of the human hand, wanted the portrait to give a clear message: that knowledge in anatomy depended on the anatomist's ability to draw. The visualization of this statement is conveyed by four hands: the hand of the dissected forearm (the object of the anatomist's observations), the anatomist's right hand holding a drawing implement (the instrument by which the anatomist can attain a better knowledge of the object), his left hand supporting a book of anatomical studies (the repository in which the anatomist preserves past and present knowledge) and the drawing of the hand (the visualization of the anatomist's knowledge). William Patch, no doubt, could draw, as could the anatomist William Cowper before him, and the anatomist William Cheselden (cat.74), after him.

William Gandy was probably trained under his father, the portraitist James Gandy; it is thought that he practised in Ireland, where he is said to have studied under Gaspar Smitz, before settling in London. He attended the Academy of c.1673 and was an artist in Lely's circle. It is possible that he was the author of the manuscript *Notes on Painting* of 1673-99; and was active in Exeter from c.1700 (Talley, 1981; Waterhouse, 1988). I.B.

William Hunter   77

MASON CHAMBERLIN (London 1727-1787)

Oil on canvas; 127 x 101.6 cm
1769

PROVENANCE: Presented by the artist in 1769

EXHIBITED: Royal Academy 1963 (76)

LITERATURE: Kemp; 1975, repr., fig.7

Royal Academy of Arts, London

William Hunter's interest in anatomy as it related to the Fine Arts was first made manifest through his lectures on anatomy at the St. Martin's Lane Academy (see Kemp, 1975, p.16). And it was no doubt owing to his continued active interest in the affairs of the Incorporated Society of Artists that Hunter was appointed first Professor of Anatomy at the Royal Academy of Arts in 1768. In this portrait Hunter holds in his hands a small bronze écorché, a version of which is included in the current exhibition (see cat.90). Indeed, among the most interesting things about the painting is the fact that Hunter was involved in the making of the plaster écorché (see cat.89) on which the small-scale model he holds, is based (Kemp, loc.

cit.). There are, in European art, a number of precedents for this type of image, where a prominent anatomist is depicted either holding, or in the presence of, an écorché figure. An early example is of the anatomist Volcher Coiter (1534-76) (Germanisches Nationalmuseum, Nuremburg). In 1789 Guillaume Voirot depicted the Professor of Anatomy at the Academy Royale, Jean-Joseph Süe, beside a reduced plaster cast of Houdon's écorché figure – a version of which also appears in Zoffany's self-portrait of c.1776 in the Uffizi. Of more direct relevance to this picture is a work of the 1760s by George Romney, of c.1768-70 (Private Collection) which depicts a man showing Spang's bronze écorché to a young student, emphasising the importance of this particular figure as an aid to anatomical education. The tradition of depicting the Royal Academy's Professor of Anatomy in the presence of the écorché was continued by John Keenan in his portrait of Hunter's successor, John Sheldon (1752-1808) (Devon and Exeter Hospitals) where a reduced plaster version of Hunter's écorché figure is shown in the background.

I am grateful to Monique Kornell for bringing the comparisons with portraits of other anatomists to my attention. M.P.

Écorché head and shoulders   78

CHARLES LANDSEER (London 1800-1879)

Red and black chalks on blue paper; 38 x 26.5 cm
Inscribed: C. *Landseer July the 18, 1815*

PROVENANCE: Unknown

LITERATURE: Venot, ed., 1976, p.15, fig.1b

Wellcome Institute Library, London

This drawing, unlike cat.80, is not taken directly from a cadaver but from the head of a plaster écorché figure in the *École Nationale Superieure des Beaux Arts de Paris*, which is traditionally ascribed to Edmé Bouchardon (1690-1762) (see Venot ed., 1976, pp.13-15, fig.1a, and Amerson, 1975, pp.382-3, figs.280-81). There is, in the Royal Academy Schools, a copy of Bouchardon's écorché figure. It is not known when the figure came into the possession of the Academy. It may have been

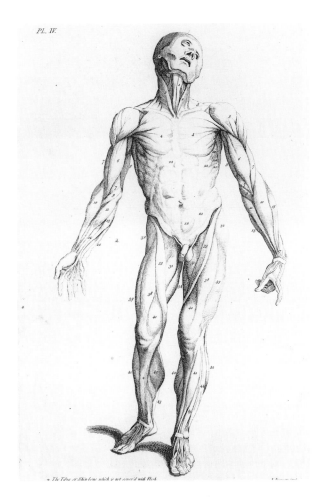

transferred there with other casts in 1768, although the existence of Hunter's écorché figure (see cat.89) may indicate that it was a later acquisition. The version of Bouchardon's écorché figure in the Royal Academy no longer has a head, although whether it had one in 1815 is open to question. In any event, as Landseer was under the tutelage of Haydon at the time he executed this drawing, it is more likely that it was made from a cast in the latter's studio. Whether Haydon owned the full cast or merely a bust-length version, as this drawing may suggest, is unknown. The use of red chalks by Landseer might suggest that the cast from which he drew was polychrome, although equally it may have been coloured to approximate more closely to his studies from actual dissections.   M.P.

Écorché figure 79

JOHN TINNEY (London ? 1707-1761)

Plate IV of *Compendium anatomicum; or a compendious treatise of anatomy adapted to the arts of Designing, Painting, and Sculpture, on Ten Folio Copper-Plates*
Inscribed: *I. Tinney sculp*
1808
Engraving; 36.4 x 21.4 cm

LITERATURE: Russell, 1974, pp.174-85

Wellcome Institute Library, London

John Tinney's *Compendious Treatise of Anatomy* was first published in 1743, and appeared in six subsequent editions until 1842 (see Russell, 1974, pp.175-7). In his preface to the first edition Tinney stressed that his book was adapted particularly to the needs of artists. He further stated: 'The best Method a young painter can follow in his Study of Anatomy is, to learn the Shape, Proportion, Situation and Manner of joining the Bones to one another; their Names; the Shapes and Situation of the Muscles ... then to compare it with some good anatomical Figure of Plaister of Paris (of which Sort there is an excellent one done by Mr. Roubilliac) and to draw from it on every side: and lastly to compare it with the Life, by setting a very muscular Man in such Attitudes as will best shew the Muscles you are in any doubt about' (quoted by Russell, 1974, p.175; for Roubilliac's anatomical figure see cat.90).

Tinney derived the plates in his book from William Cowper's *Myotomia reformata: or a New Administration of all the Humane Muscles of Humane Bodies*, of 1694 and from Vesalius – from which this engraving is taken. In the 19th century Tinney's book was still among the standard works on anatomy used by artists – much to the dismay of Benjamin Robert Haydon, who wrote on 17 November 1817: 'Why have not historical painters hitherto succeeded? They just go to the Academy, study Tinney's Anatomy, just know that there is a muscle called biceps in the arm, rectus in the thigh, pectoralis in the breast; begin an historical picture, expose it for sale, which no body is weak enough to purchase' (Pope, 1960, vol.2, p.144).   M.P.

Three Skulls, left lateral, facial and dorsal views 80

Attributed to JACOBUS SCHIJNVOET

Oil on canvas; 29 x 48 cm
Late 1720s

PROVENANCE: Presumably given by Mrs Cheselden to the College in 1753

LITERATURE: Clift, 1820, no.23; LeFanu, 1960, p.86, no.259

Royal College of Surgeons, London

This picture is part of a series of seven paintings of human skulls in the collection of the Royal College of Surgeons (LeFanu,

1960, pp.86-87, nos. 259-65). The series is related to the illustrations of Cheselden's *Osteographia* of 1733: the left lateral view in the *Three Skulls* corresponds to plate 6, fig.1, in reverse. The minutes of the College record (3 May 1753), that 'Mrs Cheselden gave three small pictures of skulls painted by Mr Cheselden himself'. Five of the paintings, including the *Three Skulls*, are unsigned, while two (LeFanu, 1960, nos. 264-65) are signed with the monogram 'I.S.' The monogram enables us to identify the painter as Jacobus Schijnvoet, a Dutch artist active in England who was employed by the anatomist William Cheselden (cat.74) to make some of the designs and engravings for *Osteographia*. Clift (1820, nos. 1, 2, 8, 19 and 23) catalogued the five unsigned paintings as the work of Cheselden. LeFanu (1960) pointed out that two paintings were signed with the monogram 'I.S.' and that they were probably the work of Schijnvoet, but he left unchanged attributions to Cheselden for the remaining five canvases. Cheselden, who subscribed to the first St. Martin's Lane Academy in 1720, was an amateur draughtsman. In *Osteographia*, he wrote that he had sometimes corrected designs and engravings executed for him by Schijnvoet and Vandegucht, and he also stated that it was necessary for an anatomist to be instructed in drawing. However, there is no mention in Cheselden's writings that he practised the art of painting. This fact and the quality of the paintings suggest that all the seven painted skulls in the collection of the Royal College of Surgeons are probably by Schijnvoet.

Little is known of Schijnvoet. Even the spelling of his name is uncertain: ('Shinevoet', 'Shindvoet', 'Schijnvoet'). According to Cheselden (1733, 'To the Reader'), he was a Dutch artist who was forced to leave his native country on account of misfortunes. Soon after he settled in England, he produced views of the interiors of cathedral churches, 'which he was forced to suffer another man to set his name to'. Later, Cheselden employed him along with Gerard Vandergucht to produce anatomical designs and engravings for his *Osteographia* of 1733. The former was responsible for most of the animal anatomies and the latter for most of the human anatomies. The last work Schijnvoet attempted before his death was the anatomy of a horse, 'which being done in the winter in his chamber without the camera (obscura)', Cheselden wrote, 'was so unequal to the rest that I could not use it'. According to the same source, Schijnvoet was a fine etcher, but less skilled as a draughtsman than Vandergucht.   I.B.

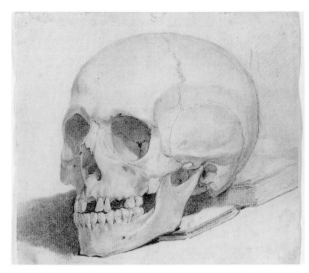

Skull, three-quarter face to left, resting on two books   81

Attributed to JACOBUS SCHIJNVOET

Black chalk on cream hand-made paper; 17.8 x 19.9 cm
? Late 1720s

PROVENANCE: presented by Rev. John Gibson to the National Gallery, 1892; transferred to the Tate Gallery, 1919

EXHIBITED: CEMA, 1944, (30) as Hogarth's *Study for the Quack Doctor*

LITERATURE: Ayrton and Denvir 1948, p.78, pl.30, as Hogarth's *Study for the Quack Doctor*, dated 1744; Davies 1959, p.56, no.104; Einberg and Egerton 1988, p.26, no.7 as *Study of a Human Skull* by an anonymous British artist, dated ? c.1750

Trustees of the Tate Gallery, London

When this drawing came into the possesion of the National Gallery collection in 1892 it was attributed to William Hogarth. This attribution was retained until it was questioned by Martin Davies (1959, no.104). Einberg and Egerton (1988, no.7) ascribed the drawing to an anonymous artist of the British School, but also raised the possibility that it could be by a Dutch or Flemish artist. The attribution to Schijnvoet of the painted skulls in the Royal College of Surgeons (cat.80) may indicate that this work is also by that artist, and may be an illustration for plate 3, fig.1, of Cheselden's *Osteographia*. This attribution is strengthened by the fact that both the drawing and the paintings in the series are anatomical studies executed under the guidance of Cheselden (cat.74). The drawing style of the Tate Gallery *Skull* is similar to that of Schijnvoet's drawings of animal anatomies in the collection of the Royal Academy (presently on loan to the Royal College of Surgeons), a style that Cheselden described as 'neat and expressive' in the preface ('To the Reader') of *Osteographia*.   I.B.

Studies of human skeleton   82

JOHN FLAXMAN

Pen and ink, and wash, on paper; 28.5 x 44 cm
Inscribed: *3 & 17 / study for plate 5*
Plate 5 of *Anatomical Studies of the Bones and Muscles, for the Use of Artists, from drawings by the late John Flaxman Esq. R.A.*, London 1833

PROVENANCE: Originally bound, with 18 other drawings, into Sir Francis Chantery's copy of Flaxman's *Anatomical Studies of the Bones and Muscles* (1833); purchased by the Royal Academy of Arts, 1885.

LITERATURE: Irwin, 1979, p.119

Royal Academy of Arts, London

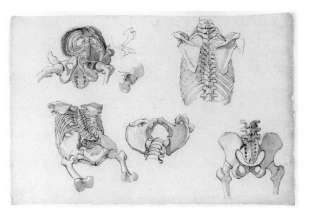

This sheet of studies is one of 19 drawings by John Flaxman, in the possession of the Royal Academy, which were engraved by Henry Landseer (Edwin Landseer's uncle) and published in 1833 as *Anatomical Studies of the Bones and Muscles for the Use of Artists*, with an introduction, and two additional plates, by William Robertson.

Flaxman had an abiding interest in anatomy, and made a serious study of the subject from the 1780s onward (see cat.88). Apart from plates illustrating the human skeleton, Flaxman included several illustrations of flayed limbs, which, as David Irwin pointed out, are not shown in the manner usually illustrated in standard anatomical treatises, but in more dramatic attitudes which would be of particular use to artists (Irwin, 1979, p.119).   M.P.

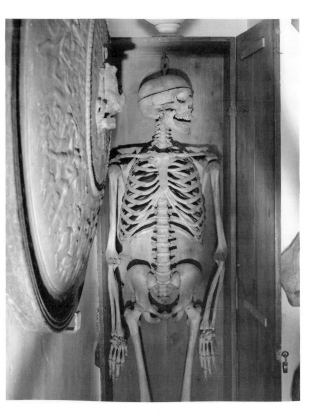

Human skeleton   83

Height, including case: 180 cm

PROVENANCE: Given to Sir John Soane in 1836 by Maria Denman, the sister-in-law of John Flaxman

LITERATURE: Irwin, 1979, p.119; Soane Museum, 1986, p.35

The Trustees of Sir John Soane's Museum, London

It is not known when John Flaxman acquired his anatomical skeleton, exhibited here. As early as 1769 however he must have observed William Hunter's demonstrations on anatomy with the aid of a human skeleton (see cat.75). Where Flaxman obtained his skeleton is again unknown although it may have been through contact with one of the surgeons connected with the Royal Academy – either Hunter himself (who died in 1783), John Sheldon, who held the post until his death in 1808, or possibly his successor, Sir Anthony Carlisle. Until the Anatomy Act was passed in 1832 it was technically illegal for anyone to procure cadavers either for dissection or to obtain skeletons – except of executed criminals. Indeed the majority of cadavers used for dissection seem to have been criminals (see e.g. cat.91). William Powell Frith, for example, recalled how, around 1824, the body of a murderer named Thurtell was dissected and various parts had casts taken from them which were used for the students at Sass's Academy (Frith, 1887, vol.1, p.183). At the same time William Mulready was informed by a friend that a surgeon whom he knew had acquired Thurtell's skeleton 'and I am informed as fine a one as was ever seen. The inspection of it will be freely granted to you' (Rorimer, 1972, 115).   M.P.

Anatomical drawing of two legs   84

BENJAMIN ROBERT HAYDON   (COL PLATE XIX)
(Plymouth 1786 - London 1846)

Pen and ink, and watercolour on paper; 46.7 x 32.3 cm
Inscribed: *These legs were done previously to my having seen a dissection, so the tendon is not correctly marked or the personeus longus and brevis [?improperly] / placed January 6th 1807 / Broad Street*
1805

PROVENANCE: Given by Haydon to his pupil David Fisher; J.H. Smith; Gilbert Stretton, who bequeathed it to the Royal Academy

Royal Academy of Arts, London

This drawing is one of a large number of anatomical studies which Haydon pasted into an album as study-aids for the pupils in his School. The drawings have recently been lifted from the album for the purposes of conservation. According to Haydon his interest in anatomy was kindled as a boy by the brother of the artist, James Northcote (Elwin, 1950, p.10). His first serious study of the subject was, however, through the study of a book of engravings after Albinus, which he purchased in Plymouth in 1803 (op. cit., p.16). In 1804, shortly after his arrival in London, Haydon bought a copy of John Bell's *Engravings explaining the Bones, Muscles, and Joints*, of 1794 (see Munby, 1937, pp.345-7), a work which profoundly influenced his belief in the importance of the first-hand study of anatomy through dissection. In the summer of 1805, after studying for a term at the Royal Academy Schools, Haydon made an intensive study of anatomy from bones and muscles borrowed from the the naval hospital in Plymouth, and from his copy of Albinus. During that time, as he later recalled, 'I got through that book of anatomical studies which all in my school have copied, from Charles Eastlake to Lance' (Elwin, 1950, p.31). On the fly-leaf of the present album Haydon wrote in 1841: 'B.R. Haydon / Begun at Plymouth / 1805 during the Academy vacation, / first Anatomical studies / From dried bones with muscles at Naval Hospital', and on the verso, 'This book was the first study of all my Pupils – who copied carefully – First Eastlake – 1808 / second Charles & Thomas Landseer – Bewick ...'

Many of the studies in the Royal Academy, including the present drawing, were produced in the summer of 1805. This

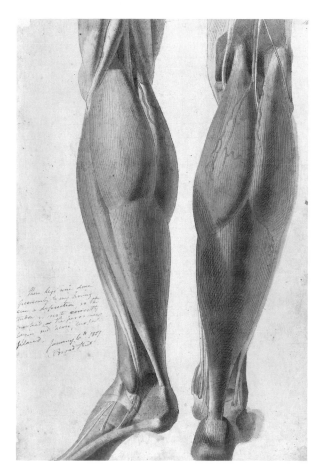

Cadaver, lying face down

(COL PLATE XX) **85**

CHARLES LANDSEER (London 1800-1879)

Red and black chalks, heightened with white on blue paper;
54.5 x 75.2 cm
Inscribed: *C. Landseer / April 28th / 18[? 15]*

PROVENANCE: Unknown

Wellcome Institute Library, London

study is probably adapted by Haydon from his copy of Albinus' *Tables of the Skeleton and Muscles of the Human Body*, because although the classical attitude of the legs and the arrangement of the muscles is similar to illustrations in Albinus (see Tab, V), Haydon has added various tendons, probably from his own observation of dried muscles.

On his return to London in Autumn 1805 Haydon moved to 3 Broad Street, Carnaby Market. He then began to examine dissected cadavers made available to him by a surgeon in Hatton Garden. 'The sight of a real body laid open', he noted, 'exposed the secrets of all the markings so wonderfully that my mind got a new and confirmed spring, the distinction between muscle, tendon, and bone was so palpable now that there could be no mistake again for ever' (Elwin, 1950, p.34). In 1806 Haydon, Wilkie, and several other students at the Royal Academy subscribed to a series of lectures on anatomy by Charles Bell. It was there, according to Haydon, 'I concluded my anatomical studies' (op. cit., p.38). By 1807, as the inscription on the present drawing indicates, Haydon could look back on his studies of 1805, and note the shortcomings in the representations of the tendons and calf-muscles (the 'peroneus longus and brevis' of the inscription). M.P.

Charles Landseer, and his brother Thomas (1798-1880) were sent by their father John Landseer to study under Benjamin Robert Haydon in 1815. Haydon had begun to take on pupils since 1809, when Charles Eastlake had come to him for instruction. 'Haydon's School', as it became in the years following 1815, adopted a curriculum which reversed current academic practice. Students began by studying and copying anatomical plates as well as Haydon's own anatomical drawings. They then moved on to the actual dissection of cadavers. Only when they understood thoroughly the principles of anatomy were they allowed to draw from the Antique – in the form of the Elgin Marbles at the British Museum. Haydon's students' practical exposure to dissection came *via* a subscription to Sir Charles Bell's anatomy classes. Bell was himself a gifted draughtsman. Indeed the present drawing is highly reminiscent of pl.1 in Bell's *A System of Dissections, Explaining the Anatomy of the Human Body, the Manner of Displaying the Parts, and their Varieties in Disease*, published in Edinburgh in 1798.

In 1864 William Bewick recalled how he had 'dissected at Sir Charles Bell's theatre of anatomy for three seasons with the Landseers. 'We dissected every part of the muscles of the body, and made drawings in red, black, and white chalk, the size of nature. These drawings were thought by the professor the finest ever made from dissection' (quoted in Cummings, 1963, p.370). In 1819 the *Annals of the Fine Arts*, a journal with which Haydon was closely associated, commented: 'Bewick and Thomas and Charles Landseer have been concluding their preparatory studies as far as concerns dissection. Three weeks they have been hanging over a putrid carcass, dissecting and drawing for 12 and 15 hours a day at a time of the year when surgeons generally give it up. They have made some capital drawings, examined every muscle, from its origin to its insertion, even to the very bones' (Cummings, loc. cit.).

Despite their early promise neither Charles nor Thomas Landseer attained the eminence of their younger brother, Edwin (1803-73). Thomas, who like his father was deaf, depended for his living chiefly on the engravings which he made from Edwin's works. Charles, who was apparently an extremely likeable and witty man, also found it difficult to attain the artistic and social heights scaled by Edwin, despite the latter's attempts to introduce him to polite society. M.P.

Écorché figure 86

JOSEPH WRIGHT (Derby 1734-97)

Sketchbook; 24 x 17 cm
Inscribed on front cover: *Jo: Wright / Book of Sketches / Feb* 1774
and below, upside down, *XII*

PROVENANCE: Presented by Edward Croft-Murray to the
British Museum in 1939

EXHIBITED: British Museum 1971 (71); Kenwood 1974 (53);
Sudbury 1987 (8); Tate Gallery 1990 (76)

LITERATURE: Egerton 1990, cat.76, p.140

The Trustees of the British Museum, London

This line drawing is one of several studies made by Wright
during his time in Rome (1773-75) from an écorché figure by
the French sculptor, Jean-Antoine Houdon (1741-1828).
Houdon, who studied in Rome from 1764 to 1768, produced his
so-called *écorché au bras tendu* in 1767 (see Reau and Vallery-
Radot, 1938, pp.170-82), and Wright's drawing is taken from
this. Houdon's *écorché au bras tendu* was produced while the
sculptor was attending the French Academy in Rome, and was
the result of intense study of dissections which he observed at
the hospital of Saint-Louis-des-Français. Houdon's reason for
modelling his écorché figure with the right arm outstretched
was based on the fact that he had been commissioned in 1766
to produce two statues of St. Bruno and St. John the Baptist. It
was in order to achieve the most faithful representation of St.
John that Houdon decided to produce an écorché figure. And
since the outstretched arm was a gesture traditionally
associated with the Baptist, Houdon also used it in his écorché
figure (op. cit., p.174). We may assume that Wright made his
drawings of Houdon's écorché figure at the French Academy in
Rome, where it was then situated. By this time however casts
were beginning to be taken from the figure, which rapidly
became regarded as one of the most important écorché figures

in Europe. Indeed, in 1775 Vien, Director of the French
Academy in Rome, instructed all students, as part of the
curriculum, to study Houdon's écorché figure (op. cit., p.180).
Small-scale versions of Houdon's figure were not however
produced until later in the 1770s (ibid.). M.P.

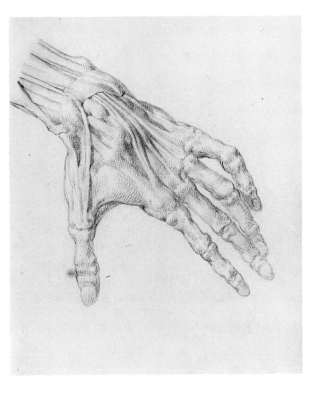

Anatomical study 87

JOHN RUSSELL (Guildford 1745 - Hull 1806)
Sketchbook; 21 x 15.2 cm

PROVENANCE: Purchased from R.B. Webb, Birmingham, 1951

City of Birmingham Art Gallery

This is one of three sketchbooks by Russell in the collection of
the City of Birmingham Art Gallery, devoted to the study of
anatomy and antique statuary. Although it is not known when
Russell began his apprenticeship, until 1767 he received
training from Frances Cotes from whom he learnt to paint both
in oils and pastels. He subsequently enrolled as a student in the
Royal Academy Schools on 17 March 1770 (Hutchison, 1962,
p.135). It has been stated (Williamson, 1903, p.28), that
Russell regularly attended William Hunter's lectures on
anatomy, an assertion which is supported by the very competent
anatomical studies in the sketchbook exhibited here, which
include drawings of muscles and skeletons.

Several of the drawings of skeletons in the sketchbook are
annotated by Russell in shorthand, probably referring to the
names of particular bones. Russell began to keep a diary in
shorthand on 6 July 1776. Unfortunately, very little of it is
available in translation – a difficulty which is compounded by
the fact that the system used by Russell (*The Universal English
Shorthand*, published by John Byrom in 1767) is no longer used.
Russell, a complex and highly sensitive individual, is best
known today for his work as a portraitist. However, he also had a
keen interest in science. And in addition to his anatomical
drawings he made a series of engravings of the lunar surface with
the aid of a telescope (British Museum, Tab.599a), which were
published in 1797, as well as illustrations for Robert Thornton's
Illustrations of the Sexual System of Linnaeus of 1799. M.P.

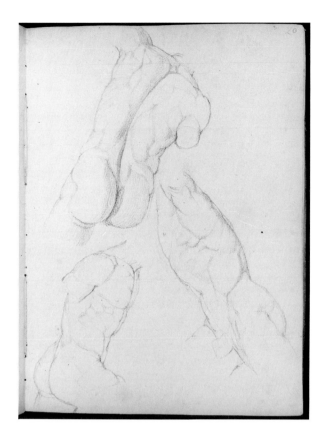

Anatomical sketchbook 88

JOHN FLAXMAN (York 1755 - London 1826)
Note and Sketchbook; 23 x 17 cm

PROVENANCE: Bequeathed to the Fitzwilliam Museum by
Charles Fairfax Murray

LITERATURE: Irwin, 1979, p.118-9; Symmons, 1984, pp.87-8

Fitzwilliam Museum, Cambridge

The studies from the *Borghese Gladiator*, shown here, form part
of a series of illustrations for an unpublished treatise by
Flaxman entitled 'Motion & Equilibrium of the Human Body'
contained within this sketchbook. The treatise is divided into
seven chapters entitled respectively, 'The Motion of the
Human Body', 'The Equilibrium', 'Anatomy', 'Proportions',
'Character', 'Drapery', and 'Composition'. The illustration
exhibited here relates to the chapter on anatomy. Flaxman
believed that although Hippocrates had studied the external
human form and the skeleton, he did not practice dissection,
and that as a consequence classical sculptors such as Phidias
and Praxiteles, unlike modern artists, did not have access to
the dissected human form. He stated (p.14) that 'they must
have made amends for that defect by a more diligent study of
the living figure under all its forms & circumstances as adjusted
by Philosophy and Geometry'. He notes further (p.15) that 'the
Anatomical divisions of figures in violent motion as the Group
of Boxers, the figure commonly called the fighting Gladiator,
their anatomical forms will be ascertained by subjects of
common nature'.

John Flaxman enrolled as a student in the Royal Academy
Schools on 7 October 1769 (Hutchison, 1962, p.134), and
must have been among the first students to listen to Dr.
William Hunter's lectures as Professor of Anatomy there.
Flaxman seems to have had an abiding interest in anatomy,
although the first real evidence that he was making a study of
the subject comes during his visit to Italy (1787-94). In July
1788 he wrote to William Hayley that he was studying

'anatomy, attitudes, and draperies' (Irwin, 1979, p.47). While
in Rome Flaxman subscribed to a series of lectures on anatomy,
and purchased a copy of the works of Hippocrates (Symmons,
1984, p.88), passages from which he evidently quotes in this
treatise. In later life Flaxman corresponded with Alexander
Munro, and in 1812 sent him, what he believed to be,
Raphael's skull. (Irwin, 1979, p.119). Although Hippocrates is
not among the texts included in the posthumous sale of
Flaxman's library at Christie's (12 June 1828) several other
important anatomical works were sold, including Charles Bell's
Anatomy of Expression, Stubb's *Anatomy of the Horse*, Munro's
Outlines of Anatomy, and works by Albinus, Brisbane, Camper,
Dürer, Eustachius, Fyfe, and Tyson. M.P.

Écorché figure 89

J.M.W. TURNER (London 1775-1851)
Black chalk on paper; 47.6 x 27.3 cm
c.1790-95

PROVENANCE: Turner Bequest; X/A

LITERATURE: Finberg, 1909, vol.1, p.14

Turner Collection, Tate Gallery, London

According to Finberg (loc. cit.) this drawing, which he says is
from a 'well-known anatomical model', was probably made by
Turner after working from the Antique, but before he entered
the Life Schools at the Royal Academy – in which case it
would date from about June 1792. However, it is probably safer
to assume that it was made during Turner's studentship,

between about 1790 and 1795. The model upon which Turner's drawing is based, is that which appears in Zoffany's *Academicians of the Royal Academy* (cat.5) and, *Dr. William Hunter lecturing at the Royal Academy* (cat.75). William Hunter was principally responsible for the production of this figure, which was made, at the request of the Society of Artists, probably in the early 1760s (see Kemp, 1975, p.16). According to an account left by Hunter's brother, John, the Society, having chosen a specimen from among the men who had recently been hanged at Tyburn, sent for William Hunter. 'As all this was done', he noted, 'in a few hours after death, and as they had not become stif [sic], Dr. Hunter conceived he might first be put into an attitude and allowed to stifen [sic] in it, which was done, and when he became stif [sic] we all set to work and by the next morning we had the external muscles all well exposed ready for making a mold from him, the cast of which is now in the Royal Academy' (Kemp, loc. cit.). Although other versions of Hunter's écorché figure were produced (see discussion in cat.91) Turner's drawing seems to have been made from the cast, as the presence of a rod supporting the left arm indicates. By the mid-1790s the figure may therefore already have been in a fragile condition. It is apparently no longer in existence, and has presumably perished. M.P.

Écorché figure (COL PLATE XXI) 90
After MICHAEL HENRY SPANG (died London 1762)
Bronze; 24.8 cm (height excl. base)
After 1761

PROVENANCE: Purchased from Mr. Alfred Spero under the terms of the John Webb Trust.

EXHIBITED: Rouen, 1977, (5)

LITERATURE: Amerson, 1975, pp.349-356; Brock, 1983, p.9; Dossie, 1782, vol.3, p.442; Graves, 1907, p.242, no.162; Gunnis, 1968, pp.292 and 361; Kemp 1983, p.383, fig 61; Rees, 1819, s.v. 'Anatomy, Picturesque'; Rouen, 1977, no.5; Smith, 1828, vol.2, p.11; Wegner, 1939, pl.63

The Board of Trustees, Victoria and Albert Museum, London

The bronze écorché model in the collection of the Victoria and Albert Museum is a small-scale version of the life-size plaster cast of an executed criminal made by William Hunter for use in his lectures on anatomy at the Royal Academy (see cats. 5, 75 and 89). This cast is dated to the 1750s on the basis of John Hunter's annotations to his brother's biography (Kemp, 1975, p.16; Brock, 1983, p.9). The bronze model, like the plaster cast, stands with its left leg bent and resting on a stump, the right arm raised above its head and the body held in a pronounced sway to the right. At least one other scale copy of the Hunter écorché existed. Ree's *Cyclopaedia* of 1819 (s.v. 'Anatomy, Picturesque') makes mention of a plaster cast three feet in height by 'Banks' and this may perhaps be identified with the 'anatomical figure' by Thomas Banks (see cat.91) listed in his sale (Christie's, 22 May 1805, lot 34). One may also note a plaster cast, slightly larger than cat.90, which appears in the background of John Keenan's portrait of John Sheldon (Royal Devon and Exeter Hospital), who followed Hunter as Professor of Anatomy at Royal Academy (Wegner, 1939, pl.63).

The écorché model originated in the 16th century and was adopted by artists and anatomists who shared an interest in the structure of the human body. The portability, relative ease of access, and incorruptible nature of the écorché model enabled it to serve as an alternative to the study of myology from a cadaver. Tinney in his *Compendium Anatomicum* of 1743

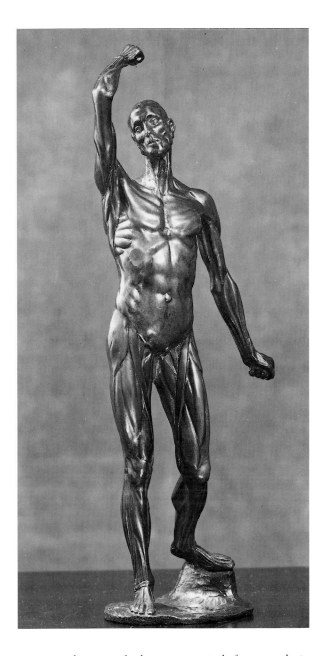

promotes the use of plaster anatomical figures and, in particular, suggests that of Roubilliac's (cat.79). An écorché by L.F. Roubilliac (c.1705-1762) was a precursor to Spang's in England. A cast identified as Roubilliac's *Anatomy* was sold in his sale in 1762 (Mr. Langford, Second Day, 13 May 1762, lot 33) and an example was once owned by George Michael Moser (Mr. Hutchins, 7 July 1783, lot 63). It was still in use, along with Spang's, in the early 19th century when it is described by Rees as 'very natural and good' (Rees, 1819, s.v. 'Anatomy, Picturesque').

It is only recently that previous attributions of this work to Francavilla and Cigoli have been rejected in favour of a dating in the 18th century (Amerson, 1975, no.47, pp.349-356; Kemp, 1965, pp.15-16). An early depiction of the cast is found in Mason Chamberlin's 1769 portrait of William Hunter (cat.77) where it is seen held by the great anatomist and collector. One owner of the bronze cast well-informed of its genesis was the sculptor and painter James Paine Jr. (1745-1829). In a list of belongings taken on a trip to Albano, 20 July 1768, is 'a little Anatomycal figure in bronze, by Spang, from a model he made in wax, from nature, of a finely proportioned Man executed at the Gallows – and dissected by Dr. Hunter for the Artists...' (National Art Library, MS.86.EE.30, fol.1;

figure so well known to every draughtsman who assisduously studies his art.' (ibid., no.4).

In 1767, Albert Pars (*fl.*1759-1768) was awarded a premium of ten guineas for casting in bronze by the Society for the Improvement of Arts for 'the Cast of an Anatomy figure after Spang' (Dossie, 1782, vol.3, p.442). The execution of a cast has also been attributed to the medallist Edward Burch (1730-1814) (Kemp, 1975, p.16; idem, 1983, p.383). The popularity of the Spang écorché is witnessed by the number of extant casts, amongst which are variations in the positioning of the arms (Amerson, 1975, cats. 41, 46; Kemp, 1975, no.9). The cast in the Science Museum (inv. 1891-1911) is one that shows the right arm bent back towards the head. The position of the right arm and the clenched left hand of a bronze écorché by Houdon, signed and dated 1776, is remarkably close to this version (Arnason, 1964, pp.18-20; idem, 1975, p.93, figs. 4b-c). The Louvre cast of the Spang écorché has the right hand resting on the head (fig. 8, Amerson, 1975, no.46). A cast in the collection of the Oxford Museum of the History of Science (inv. 33-60), which although having lost its feet and upper right arm is still recognisable as the Spang écorché, shows the left arm set closer to the body. The raised arm of the work exhibited here allows the unobstructed display of the muscles of the torso and is also seen in earlier models, such as Cigoli's well-known écorché of *c.*1598-1600 (fig.7; see also Holman, 1977-1978).

I would like to thank Malcolm Baker and Martin Postle for bibliographic help in preparing this entry.   Monique Kornell

Anatomical Crucifixion   91

THOMAS BANKS (London 1735-1805)

Plaster cast on wooden cross; height 231.2 cm

PROVENANCE: Thomas Banks, 1801; Royal Academy Schools; J.C. Carpue 1822, on loan to William Behnes; Royal Academy Schools from *?c.*1846

LITERATURE: Bryant, 1991 (forthcoming)

Royal Academy of Arts, London

This macabre écorché, cast from the body of a Chelsea pensioner, suspended and stretched as if from the effects of crucifixion, is the result of a bizarre experiment. In 1801, Benjamin West, Thomas Banks and Richard Cosway were discussing the anatomical inaccuracies of past depictions of the crucified Christ. The basic fault, they believed, lay in artists' habit of studying only the life model or stiff corpse. Truth, they concluded, could only be achieved through observing the freshly stretched limbs of a crucified figure, in which the musculature revealed the transition from life to death.

The three Academicians approached the eminent anatomist Joseph Constantine Carpue (who in the same year published his *Description of the Muscles of the Human Body*). He recorded their singular proposal; 'three of the greatest men of their time, namely, Mr West, President of the Royal Academy, Mr Banks, and Mr Cosway... requested me to nail a subject on a cross, saying, that the tale told of Michael Angelo and others was not true of their having stabbed a man tied to a cross, and then making a drawing of the effect. Shortly after this application, a circumstance occured at the college of Chelsea, which enabled me to comply with their request' (Lancet, 1846, p.167). One precendent the three artists may have had in mind is Michelangelo's crucifix made for the church of Santo Spirito in Florence (1494; now Casa Buonarotti, Florence) for which the monastery, according to Vasari 'placed some rooms at his diposal where Michelangelo very often used to flay dead bodies in order to discover the secrets of anatomy' (Vasari, 1965, p.333).

Fig.7 LUDOVICO CIGOLI *Bronze Écorché*
Victoria and Albert Museum

noticed by Anthony Radcliffe and published by Kemp, 1983, p.383). Michael Henry Spang (d.1762) (Gunnis, 1968, p.361) was a sculptor of Danish origin who executed decorative sculptural work for Robert Adam. There is a signed bronzed terracotta statuette of Hogarth by him in the Victoria and Albert Museum (inv. 311-1885). The 1761 exhibition of the Society of Artists included a wax model of an 'anatomical figure' by Spang (Graves, 1907, p.242, no.162) which has been identified with the wax model in the Hunterian Museum, Glasgow (Christie's, London, 8 December 1981, lot 220; Kemp, 1983, p.383, fig.61). In its early history, the bronze écorché model remained clearly associated with Spang (otherwise known as 'Spong'). In addition to Paine's description, it is identified as 'Spong's anatomy figure in bronze, repaired by G.M. Moser' in the latter's sale of 1783 (Mr. Hutchins, Third Day, May 1783, lot 19). Ree's *Cyclopaedia* identifies 'Mr. Spong' as having made a small-scale model from Hunter's life-size écorché, and notes that the bronze casts made from it are 'excellent' for their size (Rees, 1819, s.v. 'Anatomy, Picturesque'). Smith in his 1828 biography of Nollekens remarks that the sculptor received drawing lessons from Spang, 'who drew the figure beautifully and with anatomical truth' (Smith, 1828, vol.2, p.11). He further noted that, 'Spang produced that small anatomical

Carpue recorded how, on 2 October, 1801, a Chelsea pensioner, Ensign James Legg, having had a dispute with a fellow pensioner, Ensign William Lamb, 'entered his bedroom with two loaded pistols, presented one to Lamb, and requested him to give him that satisfaction that one solder had a right to demand from a fellow solider. Lamb indignantly threw the pistol on the ground, when Legg fired the other pistol, and shot Lamb through the thorax. He immediately expired'. (Lancet, op.cit.) After Legg's trial and hanging, Carpue successfully applied to the surgeon of Chelsea Hospital for the cadaver: 'A building was erected near the place of execution; a cross provided; the subject was nailed on the cross; the cross suspended; when the body, being warm fell into the position that a dead body must fall into, let the cause of death be what it may. When cool, a cast was made, under the direction of Mr Banks, and when the mob had dispersed, it was removed to my theatre' (ibid.).

The experiment confirmed the artists' suspicions that painters of the Crucifixion hitherto had not approached reality. The hands in particular, stretched by the weight suspended from them, prompted West to remark that 'he had never before *seen the human hand*'. (Art Union, 1845, p.14) However, despite the three artists' bold criticism of past masters, one cannot assume that this was a unique and pioneering experiment in the history of art. Grunewald's *Crucifixion* from the Isenheim altarpiece (Unterlinden Museum, Colmar), for example, certainly implies first-hand knowledge of a stretched suspended corpse. The closest-known comparison, an anatomical study traditionally attributed to Alessandro Allori (Uffizi Gallery, Florence) possesses an elegance that certainly suggests a horizontally posed écorché,

but it also reveals a late Renaissance preference for idealisation quite appropriate to the spiritual nature of the subject, (Ciardi and Tomasi, 1934, p.86, fig.35).

Banks produced two casts; one from the naked figure and one after the figure had been flayed by Carpue. The first cast is now untraced. He displayed one or both of the casts in his studio in Newman Street which 'for a length of time, was resorted to by crowds of persons for the purpose of examining it'. (Art Union, loc. cit.). One of the first artists to sketch it was William Mulready either during his year as a student in Banks's studio or at the Academy Schools. Clearly the sculptor's contribution was forgotten in the 19th century, for F.G. Stephens recorded Mulready as sketching from 'Roubilliac's Anatomical Figure'. (Stephens, 1890, p.212, and see cat.90).

Both casts entered the Academy Schools, but, according to the *Art Union*, they were 'removed when George IV sent to the Academy the casts from the antique statues which had been prepared and sent to him as a present by the Pope'. (Art Union, loc. cit.). The Minutes of the Royal Academy Council meeting for 30 December 1822 reveal that Carpue successfully applied for the removal of 'two casts from a criminal fix'd to cross presented to the Academy some years since by Mssrs Cosway, Banks & himself, ... to place the same in his Museum for the advantage of students in Anatomy'. (R.A. Council Minutes, VI, p.318 & General Assembly Minutes, III, p.389, 10 February 1823).

Carpue placed the cast of the unflayed figure on loan to the sculptor William Behnes, but threatened to present it to the King of Bavaria unless some British institution offered it a home. The date at which the écorché returned to the Academy is unknown. It is next recorded in the Academy Minutes for 20 November 1917, shortly after surviving a near escape from a Zeppelin's bomb; 'H.R.H. Princess Louise, Duchess of Argyll, had consented to allow a copy of her cast of the "Anatomical Crucifixion" to be taken in order to replace or repair the cast damaged in the schools' (ibid. XX, II, p.492).

Thomas Banks's own contribution to this experiment would have been more than simply a practical response. He was repeatedly elected Visitor in the Academy Schools from 1793, and was an unsuccessful candidate for the post of Keeper in 1804, largely due to his poor health and radical political sympathies. His commitment to teaching was such that in 1802 his pupils at the Schools were eliminated from the Silver Medal competition following the discovery that Banks 'had been down to the Academy – and contrary to the express rule, had given them instruction' (Farington, V, p.1944). The catalogue of the sale of Banks' studio contents, held by Christie's on 22 May 1805, lists numerous mixed lots of antique and life casts, including five anatomical figures ('one modelled by Mr. Banks') and a sixth, of a horse. Like Flaxman, Deare and other neo-classical sculptors, Banks' interest in anatomy extended beyond reverence for the Antique. In producing this unusual écorché, he was, in effect, disproving a legend and surpassing Michelangelo.   Julius Bryant

(Shown at Kenwood only)

Bibliography

Allan 1968 D.G.C. Allan, *William Shipley, Founder of the Royal Society of Arts, A Biography with Documents*, London, 1968.

Allen 1984 Brian Allen, *Francis Hayman and the English Rococo*, Ph.D. thesis, Courtauld Institute of Art, University of London, 1984.

Allen 1987 Brian Allen, *Francis Hayman*, exhibition catalogue, the Iveagh Bequest, Kenwood, 1987.

Amerson 1975 L.P. Amerson Jr., *The Problem of the Écorché: a Catalogue Raisonne of Models and Statuettes from the Sixteenth Century and Later Periods*, Ph.D thesis, Pennsylvania State University 1975; Ann Arbor, U.M.I. 1976.

Andrews and Brotchie 1960 Keith Andrews and J.R. Brotchie, *Catalogue of Scottish Drawings, National Gallery of Scotland*, Edinburgh, 1960.

Angelo 1904 Henry Angelo, *The Reminiscences of Henry Angelo*, 2 vols., London, 1904.

Arnason 1964 H.H. Arnason, *Sculpture by Houdon*, exhibition catalogue, Worcester, Mass., 1964.

Arnason 1975 H.H. Arnason, *The Sculpture of Houdon*, London, 1975.

Arts Council 1960 *Johan Zoffany*, exhibition catalogue, 1960.

Arts Council 1961 *Royal Academy Diploma Pictures, 1768-1851*, exhibition catalogue, Royal Academy of Arts, London, 1961.

Arts Council 1962 *British Self-Portraits*, exhibition catalogue, 1962.

Arts Council 1972 *The Age of Neo-Classicism*, exhibition catalogue, Royal Academy of Arts and Victoria and Albert Museum, London, 1972.

Ashmole 1964 B. Ashmole, *The Classical Ideal in Greek Sculpture*, Semple Lectures, University of Cincinatti, 1964.

Ayrton and Denvir 1948 Michael Ayrton and Bernard Denvir, *Hogarth's Drawings*, London, 1948.

Bailey 1974 Brian J. Bailey, *William Etty's Nudes*, Bedford, 1974.

Barr and Ingamells 1973 Bernard Barr and John Ingamells, *A Candidate for Praise, William Mason 1725-97, Precentor of York*, exhibition catalogue, York, 1973.

Barry 1775 James Barry, *An Inquiry into the Real and Imaginary Obstructions to the Acquisition of the Arts in England*, London, 1775.

Barry 1809 *The Works of James Barry*, Edward Fryer ed., 2 vols., London, 1809.

Beal 1978 Mary Beal, *Richard Symonds' Note Books*, Ph.D. thesis, Courtauld Institute of Art, University of London.

Beckett 1951 R.B. Beckett, *Lely*, London 1951.

Beckett I-VI R.B. Beckett, ed., *John Constable's Correspondence*, Suffolk Records Society, 6 vols (I-VI), 1962-68.

Bennett and Stevenson 1978 Helen Bennett and Sara Stevenson, *Van Dyck in Check Trousers, Fancy Dress in Art and Life 1700-1900*, exhibition catalogue, Scottish National Portrait Gallery, 1978.

Bignamini 1978 Ilaria Bignamini, *Mercanti, signori e pezzenti nelle stampe di William Hogarth*, Milan, 1978.

Bignamini 1986 Ilaria Bignamini, 'Jean-Bernard Le Blance a l'academie anglaise de 1748', *Revue de l'Art*, 73, pp.17-27.

Bignamini 1986-87 Ilaria Bignamini, 'The "Academy of Art" in Britain before the foundation of the Royal Academy in 1768', in Boschloo et al., 1986-87, pp, 434-50.

Bignamini 1988A Ilaria Bignamini, *The Accompaniment to Patronage, A study of the origins, rise and development of an institutional system for the arts in Britain 1692-1768*, Courtauld Institute of Art, University of London, 1988.

Bignamini 1988B Ilaria Bignamini, 'Art institutions in London, 1689-1768. A study of clubs and academies; 1, The Virtuosi of St. Luke, 1689-1743; 2, The Rose and Crown Club, c. 1704-45; 3, The Academy in Great Queen Street, 1711-20; 4, The first St. Martin's Lane Academy, 1720-24; 5. The second St. Martin's Lane Academy, 1735-68; 6, Institutions and the artist's profession', *The Walpole Society*, LIV, 1988/91.

Bignamini 1989 Ilaria Bignamini, 'Gran Bretagna: primi passi vreso il disegno industriale', in Enrico Castelnuovo, ed., *Storia del disegno industriale, 1750-1850, L'eta della rivoluzione industriale*, pp. 130-47, Milan, 1980.

Bignamini 1990 Ilaria Bignamini, 'Osservazioni sulle istituzioni il pubblico e il mercarto delle arti in Inghilterra', *Zeitschrift fur Kunstgeschichte*, 54, 2, pp. 177-97.

Bindman 1977 David Bindman, *Blake as an Artist*, Oxford 1977.

Bindman 1981 David Bindman, *Hogarth*, London 1981.

Bindman 1982 David Bindman, *William Blake: His Art and Times*, exhibition catalogue, Yale Center for British Art and Art Gallery of Ontario, 1982.

Binyon 1898-1907 Lawrence Binyon, *Catalogue of Drawings by British Artists and Artists of Foreign Origin working in Great Britain, preserved in the Department of Prints and Drawings in the British Museum*, 4 vols., London, 1898-1907.

Blankert 1982 Albert Blankert, *Ferdinand Bol (1616-1680), Rembrandt's pupil*, Doornspijk, 1982.

Blunt 1959 Anthony Blunt, *The Art of William Blake*, New York and London, 1959.

Bober and Rubinstein 1986 Phyllis Pray Bober and Ruth Rubinstein, *Renaissance Artists and Antique Sculpture*, London, 1986.

Böime 1971 Albert Böime, *The Academy and French Painting in the Nineteenth Century*, New Haven and London, 1971.

Bolten 1985 Jaap Bolten, *Method and Practice, Dutch and Flemish Drawing Books 1600-1750*, Landau Pfaiz, 1985 (1st Dutch edn. 1979).

Boschloo et al, 1989 Anton W.A. Boschloo, Elwin J. Hendrikse, Letitia C. Smit, Gert Jan van der Sman, eds., *Academies of Art between Renaissance and Romanticism*, Leids Kunsthistorisch Jaarboek, V-VI, 1986-87, 's-Gravenhage, 1989.

British Council 1966 *18th-19th Century British Painting for Europe*, exhibition catalogue, 1966.

British Council, 1977 *British Painting 1600-1800*, exhibition catalogue, Melbourne, 1977.

Brock 1983 C.H. Brock, ed., *William Hunter 1718-1783. A Memoir by Samuel Foart Simmons and John Hunter*, Glasgow 1983.

Brown 1982 D.B. Brown, *Ashmolean Museum, Oxford, Catalogue of the Collection of Drawings, Volume IV: Early English Drawings*, Oxford 1982.

Brown 1983 D.B. Brown, *Early English drawings from the Ashmolean Museum*, exhibition catalogue, Morton Morris & Co., London, 1983.

Brown 1990 D.B. Brown, *The Art of J.M.W. Turner*, London, 1990.

Bryant 1991 Julius Bryant, 'Banks's Anatomical Crucifixion', *Apollo*, June, 1991.

Burke 1943 Joseph Burke, 'A Classical Aspect of Hogarth's Theory of Art', *Journal of the Warburg and Courtauld Institutes*, VI, pp. 151-53.

Burke 1955 William Hogarth, *The Analysis of Beauty with the rejected passages from the manuscript drafts and Autobiographical Notes*, edited, with an introduction by Joseph Burke, Oxford, 1955.

Campbell 1969 J. Patricia Campbell, 'When Dutch Art came to Scotland', *Country Life*, CXLVI, August 1969, pp. 398-400.

Campbell 1979 J. Patricia Campbell, *A Catalogue and Assessment of drawings by Sir David Wilkie*, Ph.D catalogue, Edinburgh University, 1979.

CEMA 1944 *Two centuries of British Drawings from the Tate Gallery*, exhibition catalogue, 1944.

Cheselden 1733 William Cheselden, *Osteographia, or The Anatomy of the Bones*, London, 1733.

Chumbley and Warrell 1989 Ann Chumbley and Ian Warrell, *Turner and the Human Figure*, exhibition catalogue, Tate Gallery, London, 1989.

Clift 1820 William Clift, *Catalogue of the Contents of the Museum of the Royal College of Surgeons in London*, London, 1820.

Collins Baker 1912 C.H. Collins Baker, *Lely and the Stuart Portrait Painters. A study of English portraiture before and after Van Dyck*, 2 vols., London, 1912.

Constable 1953 W.G. Constable, *Richard Wilson*, London, 1953.

Cook 1984 B.F. Cook, *The Townley Marbles*, London, 1985.

Constable 1975 Freda Constable, *John Constable 1776-1837. A biography*, 1975.

Cope 1953 Zachary Cope, *William Cheselden, 1688-1752*, Edinburgh and London, 1953.

Cormack 1989 Malcolm Cormack, *Bonington*, Oxford, 1989.

Cristall 1975 Basil Taylor, *Joshua Cristall (1768-1847)*, exhibition catalogue, Victoria and Albert Museum, London, 1975.

Croft-Murray and Hulton 1960 Edward Croft-Murray and Paul Hulton, *Catalogue of British Drawings in the British Museum; 16-17th Centuries* (supplemented by Christopher White), 2 vols., London, 1960.

Croft-Murray 1962-70 Edward Croft-Murray, *Decorative Painting in England 1537-1837*, 2 vols., London, 1962-70.

Crouther Gordon 1951 T. Crouther Gordon, *David Allan of Alloa 1744-1796, The Scottish Hogarth*, Alva, 1951.

Crown 1977 Patricia Crown, *Edward Burney, An Historical Study in English Romantic Art*, Ph.D, University of California, Los Angeles, 1977.

Cummings 1963 Frederick Cummings, 'B.R. Haydon and his School', *Journal of the Warburg and Courtauld Institutes*, XXVI, 1963, pp. 367-80.

Cummings 1964 Frederick Cummings, 'Charles Bell and the "Anatomy of Expression"', *Art Bulletin*, XLVI, 1964, pp. 191-2;3.

Cunningham 1843 Allan Cunningham, *The Life of Sir David Wilkie*, 3 vols., London, 1843.

Darlington 1986 Anne Darlington, 'The Teaching of Anatomy at the Royal Academy of Arts, 1768-1782 (1)', *Journal of Art and Education*, vol. 5, No. 3, pp. 263-71.

Davies 1959 Martin Davies, *National Gallery Catalogues: The British School* (1st edn. 1946), London, 1959.

Denvir 1983 Bernard Denvir, *The eighteenth century: art, design and society, 1689-1789*, London, 1983.

DBI *Dizionario biographico degli italiani*, Rome, 1960-.

DBVI A *Dictionary of British Visitors to Italy during the Eighteenth Century based on the Archive compiled by Sir Brinsley Ford*, currently in preparation for the Paul Mellon Centre for Studies in British Art.

De Grazia 1984 Diane de Grazia, *Le Stampe dei Carracci con i disegni, le incisioni, le copie, e i dipinti connessi, Catalogo critico*, Bologna, 1984.

Delpratt Harris 1922 J. Delpratt Harris, *The Royal Devon and Exeter Hospital*, Exeter, 1922.

Detroit and Philadelphia 1968 *Romantic Art in Britain, Paintings and Drawings, 1760-1860*, exhibition catalogue, Detroit Institute of Art and Philadelphia Museum of Art, 1968.

Dobai 1968 Johannes Dobai, 'William Hogarth and Antoine Parent', *Journal of the Warbourg and Courtauld Institutes*, XXXI, 1968, pp. 336-82.

Dobson 1902 A. Dobson, *William Hogarth*, London, 1902.

Dossie 1782 R. Dossie, *Memoirs of Agriculture, and other Oeconomical Arts*, 3 vols., London 1868-82.

Dubuisson 1924 A. Dubuisson, *Richard Parkes Bonington. His Life and Work*, 2 vols., London 1924.

Duval and Cuyer 1898 M. Duval and Cuyer 1898, E. *Historie de l'anatomie plastique*, Paris 1898.

Douwes 1981 *The Rembrandt Years*, exhibition catalogue, Douwes Fine Art, May 1981.

Dumaitre 1982 Paul Dumaitre, *La curieuse destinee des planches anatomique de Gérard de Lairesse peintre en Hollande, Lairesse, Bildoo, Cowper*, Amsterdam, 1982.

Earle 1989 Peter Earle, *The Making of the English Middle Class, Business, society, and family life in London 1660-1730*, London, 1989.

Einberg and Egerton 1988 Elizabeth Einberg and Judy Egerton, *The Age of Hogarth, British painters born 1675-1709*, Tate Gallery Collections, Volume Two, London, 1988.

Egerton 1990 Judy Egerton, *Wright of Derby*, exhibition catalogue, Tate Gallery, London, 1990.

Elwin 1950 *The Autobiography and Journals of Benjamin Robert Haydon*, Malcolm Elwin ed., London, 1950.

Evans 1990 Mark Evans, *The Royal Collection: Paintings from Windsor Castle*, exhibition catalogue, National Museum of Wales, 1990.

Farington I-XVI *The Diary of Joseph Farington*, Kenneth Garlick and Angus Macintyre ed., vols. I-VI; Kathryn Cave ed., vols. VII-XVI, New Haven and London 1978-84.

Farr 1958 Dennis Farr, *William Etty*, London 1958.

Finberg 1909 A.J. Finberg, *A Complete Inventory of the Drawings of the Turner Bequest*, 2 vols., London 1909.

Fleming 1956 John Fleming, 'Allan Ramsay and Robert Adam in Italy', *Connoisseur*, March 1956, pp. 79-84.

Fleming-Williams 1975 *John Constable: Further Documents and Correspondence*, Part 2, ed., Ian Fleming-Williams, Suffolk Records Society, 1975.

Ford 1951 Brinsley Ford, *The Drawings of Richard Wilson*, London, 1951.

Ford 1963 Brinsley Ford, 'Thomas Patch: A Newly Discovered Painting', *Apollo*, vol. 77, March 1963, pp. 172-76.

Friedman and Clifford 1974 T. Friedman and T. Clifford, *The Man at Hyde Park Corner, Sculpture by John Cheere, 1709-1789*, exhibition catalogue, Temple Newsam, Leeds and Marble Hill House, London, 1974.

Frith 1887 W.P. Frith, *My Autobiography and Reminiscences*, 3 vols., London 1887.

Fraser 1986 Flora Fraser, *Beloved Emma, The Life of Emma Lady Hamilton*, London, 1986.

Gage 1987 John Gage, *J.M.W. Turner 'A Wonderful Range of Mind'*, New Haven and London, 1987.

Galt 1820 John Galt, *The Life and works of Benjamin West, Esq., President of the Royal Academy of London, Subsequent to his Arrival in this Country: Composed from Materials Furnished by Himself... Part II* London, 1820.

George D.M. George, *Catalogue of Political and Personal Satires, Department of Prints and Drawings, British Museum*, vols. V-XI, London 1935-54.

George 1948 Eric George, *The Life and Death of Benjamin Robert Haydon 1786-1846*, Oxford, 1948.

Gere and Turner 1983 J.A. Gere and Nicholas Turner, *Drawings by Raphael*, exhibition catalogue, British Museum, London, 1983.

Gilchrist 1855 Alexander Gilchrist, *Life of William Etty*, 2 vols., London, 1855.

Gilchrist 1880 Alexander Gilchrist, *Life of William Blake*, 2 vols., London, 1880 (2nd edn; 1st edn., 1863).

Glasgow 1990 *Glasgow's Glasgow. A City within a city*, exhibition catalogue, Glasgow, 1990.

Graves 1875 Algernon Graves, *The British Institution, 1806-1867*, London, 1875 (reprinted Bath, 1969).

Graves 1907 A. Graves, *The Society of Artists of Great Britain 1760-91, The Free Society of Artists 1761-1783. A Complete Dictionary of Contributors and their work from the Foundation of the Societies to 1791*, London 1907.

Gray 1935 *The Correspondence of Thomas Gray*, ed, P. Toynbee and L. Whibley, 3 vols., Oxford, 1935 (revised 1971).

Grego 1880 Joseph Grego, *Rowlandson the Caricaturist, A Selection from the Works with anecdotial descriptions of his caricatures*, 2 vols., London, 1880.

Gunnis 1968 Rupert Gunnis, *Dictionary of British Sculptors 1660-1851*, revised edition, London, 1968.

Hamilton 1874 Edward Hamilton, *A Catalogue Raisonné of the Engraved Works of Sir Joshua Reynolds*, P.R.A., *from 1755 to 1820*, London, 1874.

Hammelmann 1975 Hanns Hammelmann, *Book Illustrators in Eighteenth-Century in England*, edited and completed by T.S.R. Boase, New Haven and London, 1975.

Hampstead Arts Centre 1966 *The Artist at Work*, exhibition catalogue, Hampstead Arts Centre, London, 1966.

Haskell and Penny 1981 Francis Haskell and Nicholas Penny, *Taste and the Antique. The lure of Classical Sculpture 1500-1900*, New Haven and London, 1981.

Hayley 1809 William Hayley, *The Life of George Romney Esq.*, London, 1809.

Hazlitt 1933 *The Complete Works of William Hazlitt in Twenty-One Volumes*, ed., P.P. Howe (Centenary edition), 21 vols., London and Toronto, 1933.

Hedley 1975 O. Hedley, *Queen Charlotte*, London, 1975.

Heleniak 1980 Kathryn Moore Heleniak, *William Mulready*, New Haven and London, 1980.

Hickman 1973 P. Hickman, 'Family Portraiture in Silhouette: The Work of Mrs Daniel 'Wray', *Country Life*, 29 November, 1973, pp. 1790-92.

Hofstede de Groot 1903 Cornelis Hofstede de Groot, *Meisterwerke der Portraetmalerei*, Esslingen, 1903.

Holloway 1989 James Holloway, *Patrons and Painters, Art in Scotland 1650-1760*. Trustees of the National Galleries of Scotland, 1989.

Holman 1977-78 B. Holman, 'Verocchio's *Marsyas* and Renaissance Anatomy', *Marsyas*, 1977-78, pp. 1-10.

Holmes 1982 Geoffrey Holmes, *Augustan England, Professions, State and Society 1680-1730*, London, 1982.

Hoozee 1979 R. Hoozee, *L'opera completa di John Constable*, Milan, 1979.

Hoppe 1933 Ragnar Hoppe, *Malaren Elias Martin*, Akad, avh, Stockholm, 1933.

Hutchison 1956 Sydney C. Hutchison, *The Homes of the Royal Academy*, London, 1956.

Hutchison 1962 Sydney C. Hutchison, 'The Royal Academy Schools, 1768-1830', *Walpole Society*, vol. XXVIII, 1962.

Hutchison 1968 Sydney C. Hutchison, *The Royal Academy of Arts, 1768-1969*, London, 1968.

Irwin 1979 David Irwin, *John Flaxman 1755-1826, Sculptor, Illustrator, Designer*, London, 1979.

Jaffé 1972 P. Jaffé, *Lady Hamilton in relation to the art of her time*, exhibition catalogue, Kenwood 1972.

Jaffé 1977 Patricia Jaffé, *Drawings by George Romney*, exhibition catalogue, Fitzwilliam Museum, Cambridge, 1977.

Jones 1946-48 Thomas Jones, 'Memoirs of Thomas Jones', *The Walpole Society*, XXXII, 1946-48.

Kemp 1975 Martin Kemp, *Dr. William Hunter at the Royal Academy of Arts*, Glasgow 1975.

Kemp 1983 Martin Kemp, 'Glasgow University, Bicentenary celebrations of Dr. William Hunter (1718-83)', *Burlington Magazine*, June 1983, pp. 380-83.

Kemp (f) Martin Kemp, '"The Mark of Truth": looking and learning in some anatomical illustrations from the Renaissance and Eighteenth century', in W. Burnum and R. Porter eds., *Medicine and the Five Senses*, proceedings of conference, Wellcome Institute for the History of Medicine, (forthcoming).

Kenwood 1972 Patricia Jaffé, *Catalogue of Lady Hamilton in relation to the art of her time*, London, 1972.

Kenworthy-Browne 1979 John Kenworthy-Browne, '"Establishing a Reputation", Joseph Nollekens: The Years in Rome, I', *Country Life*, 7 June 1979, pp. 1844-48; '"Genius Recognised", Joseph Nollekens: The Years in Rome II', *Country Life*, 14 June 1979, pp. 1930-31.

Keynes 1927 Geoffrey Keynes, *Pencil Drawings by William Blake*, 1927.

Keynes 1949 Geoffrey Keynes, *Blake Studies, Notes on his life and works in seventeen chapters*, London, 1949.

Keynes 1969 Geoffrey Keynes, *Blake: Complete Writings*, Oxford, 1969 (1st edn., 1957).

Kitson 1968 Michael Kitson, 'Hogarth's "Apology for Painters"', *The Walpole Society*, XLI, 1956-68, pp. 46-111.

Kraemer 1975 Ruth S. Kraemer, *Drawings by Benjamin West and his son Raphael Lamar West*, New York, 1975.

Lambert 1981 Susan Lambert, *Drawing, Technique & Purpose*, exhibition catalogue, Victoria and Albert Museum, London, 1981.

Lambert 1984 Susan Lambert, *Drawing, Technique & Purpose, an introduction to looking at Drawings*, London, 1984.

Larsen 1986 Erik Larson, *The Paintings of Anthony Van Dyck*, 2 vols., Freren, 1986.

LeFanu 1960 William LeFanu, *A Catalogue of the Portraits and other Paintings, Drawings and Sculpture in the Royal College of Surgeons of England*, Edinburgh and London, 1960.

Leslie 1937 C.R. Leslie R.A., *Memoirs of the Life of*

Constable R.A., edited and enlarged by the Hon. Andrew Shirley, London, 1937.

Leslie and Taylor 1865 C.R. Leslie and Tom Taylor, *Life and Times of Sir Joshua Reynolds*, 2 vols., London, 1865.

MacAndrew 1978 Hugh MacAndrew, 'A Group of Batoni Drawings at Eton College, and some Eighteenth-Century Italian Copyists of Classical Sculpture' *Master Drawings*, 1978.

Manners and Williamson 1920 Lady Victoria Manners and G.C. Williamson, *Zoffany, R.A. His Life and Works, 1735-1810*, London and New York, 1920.

Manners and Williamson 1924 Lady Victoria Manners and G.C. Williamson, *Angelica Kauffmann R.A., Her Life and Works*, London, 1924.

MacDonald 1989 M.F. MacDonald, *British Artists at the Accademia del Nudo in Rome*, in Boschloo et al., *Academies of Art between Renaissance and Romanticism*, 's-Gravenhage 1989, pp. 77-94.

Millar 1969 Oliver Millar, *The Later Georgian Pictures in the Collection of Her Majesty the Queen*, 2 vols., London, 1969.

Millar 1978 Oliver Millar, *Sir Peter Lely 1618-80*, exhibition catalogue, National Portrait Gallery, London, 1978.

Morgan 1973 H. Cliff Morgan, 'The Schools of the Royal Academy', *British Journal of Educational Studies*, vol. XXI, 1973, pp. 88-103.

Morris 1925 R.B. Morris, *Devon and Cornwall Notes and Queries*, 2nd series, vol. 13, 1925.

Munby 1937 A.N.L. Munby, 'B.R. Haydon's Anatomy Book', *Apollo*, XXVI, December 1937, pp. 345-7.

Murdoch 1985 Tessa Murdoch, catalogue entry on the 'Life drawing class said to be the St. Martin's Lane Academy', in Museum of London, 1985, p. 196, no. 281.

Murray 1980 Peter Murray, *Dulwich Picture Gallery. A Catalogue*, London, 1980.

Museum of London 1985 *The Quiet Conquest: the Huguenots 1685 to 1995*, exhibition catalogue, Museum of London, 1985.

Nicolson 1968 Benedict Nicolson, *Joseph Wright of Derby, Painter of Light*, 2 vols., London, 1968.

Nottingham 1959 *Diploma Paintings* (from the Royal Academy of Arts), exhibition catalogue, University Art Gallery, Nottingham, 1953.

Oppé 1948 A.P. Oppé, *The Drawings of William Hogarth*, London, 1948.

Oppé 1950 A.P. Oppé, *English Drawings, Stuart and Georgian Periods, In the Collection of His Majesty the King at Windsor Castle*, London, 1950.

Oxford and London 1985 *Sir David Wilkie, Drawings and Sketches in the Ashmolean Museum*, exhibition catalogue, Ashmolean Museum, Oxford, and Morton Morris and Company Ltd, London, 1985.

Paley 1978 Morton D. Paley, *William Blake*, 1978.

Paris 1989 *Jacques-Louis David 1749-1825*, exhibition catalogue, Louvre and Versailles, Paris, 1989.

Paris and Rome 1987 *Subleyras 1699-1749*, exhibition catalogue, Musee du Luxemburg and Accademia di Francia a Roma, Villa Medici, 1987.

Parris et al 1976 Leslie Parris, Ian Fleming-Williams, Conal Shields, *Constable, Paintings, Watercolours & Drawings*, exhibition catalogue, Tate Gallery, London, 1976.

Pasquin 1796 A. Pasquin (pseud. of J. Williams), *An Authentic History of the professors of painting, sculpture & architecture ... To which are added, Memoirs of the Royal Academicians*, London, 1796.

Paulson 1971 Ronald Paulson, *Hogarth: His Life, Art, and Times*, 2 vols., New Haven and London, 1971.

Paulson 1989 Ronald Paulson, *Hogarth's Graphic Works*,

2 vols., London, 1989 (1st edn., 1965).

Penny 1986 *Reynolds*, exhibition catalogue, Royal Academy of Arts, London, 1986.

Pevsner 1940 Nikolaus Pevsner, *Academies of Art, Past and Present*, Cambridge, 1940 (reprinted New York 1973).

Phillips 1964 Hugh Phillips, *Mid-Georgian London*, London, 1964.

Pomfret 1805 F. Seymour, *Correspondence between Frances, Countess of Hartford ... and Henrietta Louisa, Countess of Pomfret*, London, 1805.

Pope 1960 *The Diary of Benjamin Robert Haydn*, 5 vols., Cambridge, Mass., 1960-1963.

Postle 1988 Martin Postle, 'Patriarchs, Prophets, and Paviours': Reynolds's Images of Old Age', *Burlington Magazine*, CXXX, October 1988, pp. 735-44.

Postle June 1990 Martin Postle 'Covered in Ignominy: Scenes of outrage at Somerset House', *Country Life*, 14 June 1990, p. 290.

Postle November 1990 Martin Postle, 'Reynolds, Shaftesbury, Van Dyck, and Dobson: sources for *Garrick between Tragedy and Comedy*', *Apollo*, November 1990, pp. 306-11.

Pressly 1981 William L. Pressly, *The Life and Art of James Barry*, New Haven and London, 1981.

Pressly 1983 William L. Pressly, *The Artist as Hero*, exhibition catalogue, Tate Gallery, London, 1983.

Queen's Gallery 1974 *George III, Collector & Patron*, exhibition catalogue, The Queen's Gallery, Buckingham Palace, London, 1974.

Reau and Vallery-Radot 1938 Louis Reau et le Dr Pierre Vallery-Radot, 'Les Deux Écorchés de Houdon', *Aesculape*, 1938, pp. 170-82.

Redgrave 1947 Richard and Samuel Redgrave, *A Century of British Painters*, Oxford, 1947 (first published 1866).

Rees 1819 A. Rees, *The Cyclopedia or Universal Dictionary of Arts, Sciences and Literature*, II, 3rd edition, London, 1819.

Reynolds 1973 Graham Reynolds, *Catalogue of the Constable Collection*, Victoria and Albert Museum, London, 1973.

Reynolds 1975 Sir Joshua Reynolds, *Disclosures on Art*, ed. Robert Wark, New Haven and London, 1975.

Robertson ed, 1985 Emily Robertson ed., *Letters and Papers of Andrew Robertson*, London, 1895.

Rogers 1985 Malcolm Rogers, catalogue entry on Lely's 'Nymphs by a Fountain', in Washington 1985, pp. 83-84, no. 20.

Rome 1986 *Annibale Carracci e i suoi incisori*, exhibition catalogue, Istituto Nazionale per la Grafica, Rome, 1986.

Romney 1830 John Romney, *Memoirs of the Life and Works of George Romney*, London, 1830.

Rorimer 1972 Anne Rorimer, *Drawings by William Mulready*, Victoria and Albert Museum, London, 1972.

Rose, 1942 F.G. Rose, 'William Etty and the Nude', *Connoisseur*, CIX, January 1942, p. 28.

Rosenthal 1983 Michael Rosenthal, *Constable, the Painter and his Landscape*, New Haven and London, 1983.

Rouen 1977 *L'Écorché*, exhibition catalogue, Musée des Beaux Arts, Rouen, 1977.

Royal Academy 1890 *Old Masters*, exhibition catalogue, London, 1890.

Royal Academy 1931 *Paintings & Sculptures in the Diploma and Gibson Galleries, Royal Academy of Arts*, London and Glasgow, 1931.

Royal Academy 1934 *British Art*, exhibition catalogue, London, 1934.

Royal Academy 1946 *The King's Pictures*, exhibition catalogue, London, 1946.

Royal Academy 1951 *The First Hundred Years of the Royal Academy 1769-1868*, exhibition catalogue, London, 1951.

Royal Academy 1960 *The Age of Charles II*, exhibition catalogue, London, 1960.

Royal Academy 1963 *Treasures of the Royal Academy*, exhibition catalogue, London, 1963.

Royal Academy 1968 *Bicentenary Exhibition*, exhibition catalogue, London, 1968.

Royal Academy 1975 *Turner 1775-1851*, exhibition catalogue, Royal Academy, London, 1975.

Rubin 1977 James Henry Rubin, *Eighteenth-Century French Life-Drawing, Selections from the Collection of Mathias Polakovits*, exhibition catalogue, The Art Museum, Princeton University, 1977.

Russell 1954 K.F. Russell, 'The Osteographia of William Cheselden', *Bulletin of the History of Medicine*, No. 1, Jan-Feb., 1954.

Russell 1974 K.F. Russell, 'John Tinney's "Compendium Anatomicum" and its Publishers', *Medical History*, vol, 18, 1974, pp. 174-85.

Russell 1976 P.M.G. Russell, *A History of the Exeter Hospitals 1170-1948*, Exeter, 1976.

Saxl and Wittkower 1948 Fritz Saxl and Rudolf Wittkower, *British Art and the Mediterranean*, Oxford, 1948.

Schupbach 1982 William Schupbach, *The Paradox of Rembrandt's 'Anatomy of Dr. Tulp'*, Wellcome Institute for the History of Medicine, London, 1982.

Scottish Arts Council 1973 Basil Skinner, *The Indefatigable Mr. Allan*, exhibition catalogue, Edinburgh, 1973.

Sée 1922 R.R.M. Sée, *Masquerier and his Circle*, London, 1922.

Shee 1809 Martin Archer Shee, *Elements of Art, a poem; in six cantos; with notes and a preface; including strictures on the state of the arts, criticism, patronage, and public taste*, London, 1809.

Shirley 1933 Andrew Shirley, 'John Constable and "The Nude"', *Connoisseur*, XCI, April 1933, pp. 213-19.

Shirley 1940 Andrew Shirley, *Bonington*, London, 1941.

Smith 1828 J.T. Smith, *Nollekens and his Times*, 2 vols., London, 1828.

Smith 1916 A.H. Smith, 'Lord Elgin and his Collection', *Journal of Hellenistic Studies*, XXXVI, 1916.

Solkin 1982 David H. Solkin, *Richard Wilson, The Landscape of Reaction*, exhibition catalogue, Tate Gallery, London, 1982.

Spencer 1964 Marion L. Spencer, *Richard Parkes Bonington (1802-28) a reassessment of the character and development of his art*, Ph.D thesis, Nottingham, 1964.

St. Andrews 1985 *Sir David Wilkie, Sketches and Studies*, exhibition catalogue, Crawford Centre for the Arts, St. Andrews, University of St. Andrews, 1985.

St. Clair 1967 William St. Clair, *Lord Elgin and the Marbles*, London, 1967.

Stainton and White 1987 Lindsay Stainton and Christopher White, *Drawing in England from Hilliard to Hogarth*, exhibition catalogue, British Museum, London, 1987.

Stephens 1890 Frederick G. Stephens, *Memorial of William Mulready R.A.*, London, 1890.

Stephens and Hawkins 1877 F.G. Stephens and Edward Hawkins, *Political and Personal Satires, Department of Prints and Drawings, British Museum*, vols. III-IV,1877-83.

Stewart 1983 J. Douglas Stewart, *Sir Godfrey Kneller and the English Baroque Portrait*, Oxford, 1983.

Sunderland 1986 John Sunderland, 'John Hamilton Mortimer, His Life and Works', *Walpole Society*, LII, 1986.

Symmons 1984 Julia Sarah Symmons, *Flaxman and Europe: The Outline Illustrations and their Influence*, unpublished Ph.D thesis, Courtauld Institute of Art, London, 1984.

Talley 1981 M.K. Talley, *Portrait Painting in England, Studies in the Technical Literature before 1700*. Published privately by the **Paul Mellon Centre for Studies in British Art, London, 1981.**

Tate 1978 *William Blake*, exhibition catalogue, Tate Gallery, London, 1976.

Tate 1982 *Paint and Painting*, exhibition catalogue, Tate Gallery, London, 1982.

Taylor 1975 Basil Taylor, *Stubbs*, Oxford, 1975.

Thompson 1961 J.F. Thompson, 'More Paintings at the British Museum', *Connoisseur*, CXLVII, pp. 189-95.

Venot ed 1976 B. Venot ed., 'L'Écorché', *Experience Pedagogique a l'École Regionale des Beaux Arts de Rouen*, Cahier No. 3, Nov. 1976.

Vertue I-VI George Vertue, 'Note Books I-VI', *Walpole Society*, vol. XVIII (1929-30), XX (1931-32), XXII (1933-34), XXIV (1935-36), XXVII (1937-38), XXIX (1940-42).

von Erffa and Staley 1986 Helmut von Erffa and Allen Staley, *The Paintings of Benjamin West*, New Haven and London, 1986.

Walker 1989 N. Walker, *Richard Parkes Bonington, Paul Sandby*, exhibition catalogue, Prinz Max Palais, Karlsruhe, Germany, 1989.

Walpole 1849 Horace Walpole, *Anecdotes of Painting in England*, ed. Ralph N. Wornum, 3 vols., London, 1849.

Walpole 1937-83 W.S. Lewis, ed., *Horace Walpole's Correspondence*, 48 vols., New Haven and London, 1937-83.

Wark 1975 Robert R. Wark, *Drawings by Thomas Rowlandson in the Huntington Collection*, San Marino, California, 1975.

Waterhouse 1981 Ellis Waterhouse, *The Dictionary of British 18th Century Painters in oils and crayons*, Woodbridge, 1981.

Waterhouse 1988 Ellis Waterhouse, *The Dictionary of 16th & 17th Century British Painters*, London, 1988.

Webster 1970 Mary Webster, *Francis Wheatley*, New Haven and London, 1970.

Webster 1977 Mary Webster, *Johan Zoffany, 1733-1810*, exhibition catalogue, National Portrait Gallery, London, 1977.

Wegner 1939 R. Wegner, *Das Anatomenbildnis*, Basel, 1939.

Williams 1952 Iolo A. Williams, *Early English Watercolours and some cognate drawings by artists born not later than 1785*, London, 1952.

Williamson 1903 G.C. Williamson, *John Russell R.A.*, London, 1903.

Whitley 1928 William T. Whitley, *Artists and their Friends in England, 1700-1799*, 2 vols., London and Boston, 1928.

Wilton 1987 Andrew Hilton, *Turner in his time*, London, 1987.

Wolstenholme and Piper 1964 Gordon Wolstenholme and David Piper, *The Royal College of Physicians of London, Portraits*, London, 1964.

Woodward 1962 John Woodward, *A Pictorial History: British Painting*, London, 1962.

York 1963 *William Etty*, exhibition catalogue, York City Art Gallery, 1963.

Yung 1981 *National Portrait Gallery. Complete Illustrated Catalogue*, compiled by K.K. Yung, ed., Mary Pettman, London, 1981.

Ziff 1973 Gert Ziff, *Johann Heinrich Fussli, 1741-1825*, 2 vols., Munich, 1973.

Photographic credits

By Gracious Permission of Her Majesty the Queen, ill.17 (Bignamini), cat.5; Ashmolean Museum, Oxford, cats. 31, 63, 69; Bradford Art Galleries and Museums, cat.1; British Museum, ills. 3-6, 8-11, 13, 15, 16 (Bignamini), ills. 6, 7, 10, 11 (Postle), cats. 25, 27, 29, 36, 41, 42, 43, 55, 56, 60a, 60b, 64, 86; Christie's, cats. 15, 67; Courtauld Institute, ill.4 (Postle), cats. 30, 32, 44, 62, 80, 87; Dulwich Picture Gallery, cat.12; Lady Lever Gallery, cat.40; Fitzwilliam Museum, Cambridge, cats. 59, 88; Forbes Magazine, cat.72; Ilaria Bignamini, ills. 12, 14 (Bignamini); National Galleries of Scotland, cats. 19, 51; National Museum of Wales, cat.48; National Portrait Gallery, cat.35; Newcastle University, cat.24; Nottingham Castle Museum and Art Gallery, cats. 21, 54; Nottingham University, cat.37; Paul Mellon Centre, ills. 1, 2 (Bignamini), ills. 1, 2, 5, 8 (Postle); cats. 2, 13, 22, 23, 38, 49, 57, 58, 61, 66, 71; Pembroke College, Cambridge, cat.33; Royal Academy of Arts, London, ills. 3, 9 (Postle), cats. 3, 4, 7, 11, 39, 46, 50, 70, 77, 82, 84, 91; Royal Academy of Arts, Stockholm, cat.6; Royal College of Physicians, cat.75; Royal Devon and Exeter Hospitals, cat. 76; Scottish National Portrait Gallery, cats. 8, 10; Sir John Soane's Museum, cat.83; Sotheby's, cat.9; Tate Gallery, cats. 28, 45, 73a, 73b, 73c, 81, 89; Victoria and Albert Museum, cats. 17, 18, 20, 26, 34, 47, 53, 68, 90; Wellcome Institute, cats. 52, 65, 74, 78, 79, 85; York City Art Gallery, cat.14.